Hebrews

Richard E. Lauersdorf

Publishing House
St. Louis

The interior illustrations were originally executed by James Tissot
(1836-1902). The drawings of the tabernacle and the ark are by NPH
artist Linda Taylor.

Commentary and pictures are reprinted from HEBREWS (The People's
Bible Series), copyright © 1986 by Northwestern Publishing House.
Used by permission.

Scripture is taken from The Holy Bible: NEW INTERNATIONAL
VERSION, © 1973, 1978, 1984 by the International Bible Society.
Used by permission of Zondervan Bible Publishers.

Copyright © 1992 Concordia Publishing House
3558 S. Jefferson Avenue, St. Louis, MO 63118-3968
Manufactured in the United States of America

1 2 3 4 5 6 7 8 9 10   01 00 99 98 97 96 95 94 93 92

CONTENTS

PREFACE

The People's Bible Commentary is just what the name implies—a Bible and commentary for the people. It includes the complete text of the Holy Scriptures in the popular New International Version. The commentary following the Scripture sections contains personal applications as well as historical background and explanations of the text.

The authors of *The People's Bible Commentary* are men of scholarship and practical insight gained from years of experience in the teaching and preaching ministries. They have tried to avoid the technical jargon which limits so many commentary series to professional Bible scholars.

The most important feature of these books is that they are Christ-centered. Speaking of the Old Testament Scriptures, Jesus himself declared, "These are the Scriptures that testify about me" (John 5:39). Each volume of *The People's Bible Commentary* directs our attention to Jesus Christ. He is the center of the entire Bible. He is our only Savior.

We dedicate these volumes to the glory of God and to the good of his people.

The Publishers

INTRODUCTION

The Author

The book of Hebrews has been called the riddle of the New Testament. Take the matter of its author for example. Nowhere in the book does he name himself or disclose his identity, though several hints are given. He indicates in 2:3 that he has not received the word of salvation firsthand from the Lord, but from "those who heard him." He seems to have moved in the circle of Paul's friends and co-workers as his words about "brother Timothy" in 13:23 indicate. His writing shows him very much at home in the Old Testament and well acquainted with the worship life and religious teachings of the Jews.

From such tantalizing hints have come many guesses about the author's identity. By the end of the second century the Apostle Paul's name had been connected with the letter. And yet Paul's different style of writing, his claim in 1 Corinthians 15:8 of having received the gospel directly from the Lord and his custom of invariably naming himself as author in his epistles seem to argue against this choice. Others have mentioned as a likely candidate Barnabas, the traveling companion of Paul, whom Acts 4:36 calls "a Levite from Cyprus."

Luther strongly suggested Apollos, whom Acts 18:24,25 describes as "a Jew . . . a learned man, with a thorough knowledge of the Scriptures . . . instructed in the way of the Lord . . . spoke with great fervor and taught about Jesus accurately." Luther's guess is as good as any, but in the end we have to agree with the early church father: "Who wrote the epistle, God only knows certainly."

The uncertainty about the author does not diminish our certainty about the book. In every part the authorship of the Holy Spirit is apparent and to him goes the appreciation for this great book. From his inspiration of the unnamed author has come a book with a vital message for every age. Beautifully and skillfully the book of Hebrews focuses on Jesus Christ as the perfect Savior from sin and the total answer for every need.

The Readers

To whom this unnamed author wrote is not clear either. The title, "To the Hebrews," found in our English Bibles, was not part of the original letter but was added later in the second century. Nor does the book itself name its readers, though again it gives certain clues. The readers were a definite group of Christians with whom the author, as indicated in 13:19, had once lived and with whom he hoped to be reunited. They had been in the faith for some time, as 5:12 shows, but were now in danger of growing stagnant. They had previously suffered persecution, as we hear in 10:32-34, but were now in danger of suffering more. They were still believers in Christ but were now in danger of turning away from him. They also seemed to be Jewish in background. The book with its many quotes from the Old Testament and its many references to the worship life of God's Old Testament people indicates readers who were well at home in such areas.

Where these readers lived is also unclear. The reference in 13:24 about "those from Italy" sending their greetings could indicate Christians originally from Italy now sending greetings back to their mother church. Also because this letter was first referred to and quoted by Roman authors, some have concluded that the original readers were Christians living in Rome.

Again, the uncertainty about the recipients does not diminish our certainty about the book. Regardless who the original readers were, this book with its strong pastoral exhortations has something to say to all believers. Who of us doesn't need the stirring call to remain moored to Christian truth, to maintain steady confidence in Christ, and to move forward in Christian maturity?

The Date

We are also unsure about the exact date of its writing. It had to be before A.D. 96, when quotations from it are found in another writing, but how much earlier is difficult to say. One clue given in the book itself is the reference to persecution. The readers had earlier suffered insult and persecution. We are told in 10:34 that some had even been imprisoned and had lost property. The persecution had not yet led to bloodshed (12:4), but was now heating up. Roman history tells us that Nero's persecution of the Christians was full blown in A.D. 64 and continued for some years. This book might well have been written during this period of persecution.

Another clue is the absence of any reference in the letter to the fall of Jerusalem. This famous city of the Jews with its beloved temple fell to the Roman legions in A.D. 70. The ruin of the temple and all that went with it would have been a convincing proof for the author's claim that Christ and his work had rendered the Old Testament sacrificial system obsolete. The lack of reference to Jerusalem's fall causes some to think that the book was written shortly before A.D. 70.

Perhaps the closest we can come is to date Hebrews somewhere in the years A.D. 64-70. But its central message of the supremacy of Christ and his work of salvation is timeless.

The Purpose

About its purpose there can be no uncertainty. It was written to urge people not to abandon their faith in Christ. In 13:22 the author himself calls it a "word of exhortation," and it reads almost sermon-like in the way certain doctrines are first explained and then applied to the lives of the people. In the first part of the epistle the author sets forth the doctrines of the supremacy of Christ and the all-sufficiency of his work. In the second part he then applies these truths to the lives of his readers. It's as if he were telling them, "Look what a supreme treasure you have in Christ and Christianity" and then asking them, "Now what are you going to do with this treasure?"

For Jewish Christians facing the temptation of turning away from Christianity and back to their Jewish religion such words were most appropriate. Christianity had been outlawed when Nero began his religious persecution, while Judaism remained legal and under state protection. The pressure to revert to the safety of Judaism was very real and grew even more so as the persecution heated up.

Some had already fallen away; others were in danger of doing so, but the author urged, "Don't." And then he told them why not, as in beautiful fashion and with intense detail he showed the supremacy of Christianity. With broad and beautiful strokes he painted the sweeping design of the Old Testament, showing how its fulfillment was found in the person and work of Christ. Again and again he used the key word "better" as he portrayed Christianity as the one true religion, the perfect and final revelation of God to man.

Some have shied away from this book as perhaps one of the most difficult in the New Testament. But what a book it is! It demonstrates the supremacy of Christ and presents him as God's perfect word to man and man's perfect representative with God. It describes Christ's ministry for the people, a ministry which is still going on in heaven today. It speaks of unshakable rest in a time when all around us is shaking in unrest. It urges the child of God not to sit down or slide backward, but to stride forward on the trail blazed by Christ. It picks the child of God up when discouraged and provides him with incentive to travel upward to the eternal home. Surely such a book has much to say to us!

The Outline

One hesitates to interrupt the flow of the book with outlining attempts. Its almost 7,000 words can be read through in less than an hour, something the reader might consider doing before proceeding. Yet outlining might help us. The first part of the epistle is doctrinal in nature (1:1-10:18), setting forth the supremacy of Christ and the sufficiency of his work. The second part is practical (10:19-13:17), urging us to apply these treasures to our daily lives. Already in the first part of the letter the author several times drives his point home with warnings and applications. But the application proper begins in the second portion, where he again and again uses the phrase, "Let us . . ." Then follows a brief conclusion (13:18-25).

    I. What a Supreme Treasure We Have in Christ (1:1-10:18)
        A. Christ Is Superior in His Person (1:1-4:13)
            1. He is superior as the perfect revelation of God (1:1-3)
            2. He is superior to the angels (1:4-2:18)
            3. He is superior to Moses (3:1-4:13)

B. Christ Is Superior in His Priesthood
   (4:14-10:18)
   1. He is a priest superior in qualifica-
      tions (4:14-6:20)
   2. He is a priest superior in office
      (7:1-28)
   3. He is a priest superior in sanctuary
      and covenant (8:1-13)
   4. He is a priest superior in sacrifice
      (9:1-10:18)
II. What We Are to Do with This Supreme Treasure (10:19-13:25)
   A. Let Us Draw Near to God in Confident
      Faith (10:19-39)
   B. Let Us Remember the Heroes of Faith
      (11:1-40)
   C. Let Us Grow in Faith Through God's
      Discipline (12:1-29)
   D. Let Us Live in Faith Toward Those
      Around Us (13:1-17)
   E. Personal Instructions and Final Greet-
      ings (13:18-25)

PART ONE

WHAT A SUPREME TREASURE
WE HAVE IN CHRIST
(1:1-10:18)

Christ Is Superior in His Person
He Is Superior As the Perfect Revelation of God

1 **In the past God spoke to our forefathers through the prophets at many times and in various ways, ²but in these last days he has spoken to us by his Son, whom he appointed heir of all things, and through whom he made the universe. ³The Son is the radiance of God's glory and the exact representation of his being, sustaining all things by his powerful word. After he had provided purification for sins, he sat down at the right hand of the Majesty in heaven.**

In all the New Testament no epistle comes more quickly to the point. Without introduction or greeting the author launches into his subject. It's as if he just could not wait to set forth the glorious superiority of Jesus Christ.

Writing to people half inclined to turn back to Judaism because of difficulty and danger, the author began with a point with which they could hardly disagree. God had indeed spoken in the past to their forefathers. At many times and in the various forms of law, history, poetry and prophecy God had spoken to them through his prophets from Moses down to Malachi. But the ministry of the prophets

7

had been partial and their message incomplete. More was to come, not to cancel what had been divinely recorded, but to complete it.

So it happened, just as the fathers had been told. Moses had told them in Deuteronomy 18:15, "The LORD your God will raise up for you a prophet like me from among your own brothers. You must listen to him." And it had happened! "In these last days," that New Testament period of time in which we live and after which comes only eternity, God has spoken in the person of his Son.

Note the stress on inspiration. Through the prophets and now through his Son, God was speaking. They spoke his words. The prophets spoke for God; the Son spoke as God. Now having spoken through his Son, God has nothing more to say to man. His Son, the Redeemer, to whom the Old Testament pointed, is the ultimate Word and the perfect Revelation of God. How foolish for anyone to turn his back on such a revelation for any reason!

Next follow a series of seven statements pointing out Christ's superiority as the perfect revelation of God. 1) At the end of all he is seen as "heir," owner and ruler of all. 2) At the beginning of all he stands as "creator," participating in that awesome act.

3) Even more, he is "the radiance of God's glory." God's glory, the whole array of his divine attributes, radiates forth in Jesus. Radiance is an inner brightness which shines out like the sun in the sky with its streaming light. To see that light is to see the sun; to see Jesus is to see the God of glory. 4) And "he is the exact representation of his being." An exact representation is some exact impression made by a tool, like a coin stamped by a die. So Jesus exactly represents the Father. To know Jesus is to know God's nature or glory. "God in focus" we might call Jesus. He expressed it

even better when he said in John 14:9, "Anyone who has seen me has seen the Father."

5) There's still more. Not only was Jesus active in creation, but he "sustains all things by his powerful word." Let the scientists theorize and test; we know who holds all things together and leads them toward their final goal. It is he whose powerful word brought all into being in the beginning. "He is before all things, and in him all things hold together," says Colossians 1:17. In the strong hands of such a Christ believers are eternally secure.

6) The sixth statement takes us to the heart of the matter. The whole letter was written to show that Christ was superior because he had come to "provide purification for sin." Sin stains; it defiles and damns. Only one could purify and only once would he need do it. At Calvary's cross the Creator and Sustainer became the Sin-bearer. Here is his most amazing glory! What a staggering thought — the sovereign Lord became the sacrificial Lamb!

With the work of redemption done, 7) "he sat down at the right hand of the majesty in heaven." "Right hand" refers to a position of power and honor; "Majesty in heaven" refers to God and all his awesome greatness. The ascended Lord Jesus holds the scepter in his nail-scarred hands, ruling over all in heaven, earth and hell. What a picture of greatness!

Tired under affliction and almost ready to call it quits because of persecution, those Jewish Christians needed such a view of the perfect and victorious Christ. So do we! Struggling to keep the faith in an increasingly hostile world, so often engaged in what seems no more than a holding action, we need eyes lifted to the Lord Jesus, who is God's perfect revelation. May what the author has shown us of his glory prompt us to say, "My Lord and my God!" (John 20:28).

He Is Superior to the Angels

⁴So he became as much superior to the angels as the name he has inherited is superior to theirs. ⁵For to which of the angels did God ever say, "You are my Son; today I have become your Father"? Or again, "I will be his Father, and he will be my Son"? ⁶And again, when God brings his firstborn into the world, he says, "Let all God's angels worship him."

In the Old Testament the Law was given through angels. In those days angels frequently appeared to God's people. So Jewish Christians would know and respect the high position of such heavenly beings. Yet Jesus ranked head and shoulders above them. He is eminently "superior" to the angels, the author tells us, using a word that is to appear again and again in Hebrews, thirteen times in all. In fact, Jesus was superior to anything and everything, and he was *their* Savior. How could they even think of leaving him?

Those Jewish Christians would also be well versed in the Old Testament Scriptures and would readily accept their authority. So the author lets the Old Testament speak. In every chapter of his letter there is at least one quotation from the Old Testament; in this chapter there are seven! Reading the quotations makes us marvel at the depth of the Old Testament.

The Messiah was at the heart and center of the whole Old Testament Scripture. He was in passages where we might not have even imagined him to be. In John 5:39 the Messiah himself told the Jews about the Old Testament, "You diligently study the Scriptures. . . . These are the Scriptures that testify about me." In Acts 10:43 Peter repeated that tremendous thought to Cornelius, "All the prophets testify about him that everyone who believes in him receives forgiveness of sins through his name." And the author of

Hebrews underscores the point! Skillfully, under the inspiration of the Holy Spirit and with the Holy Spirit as interpreter, he shows how the Old Testament testified of Christ. The first quotation is from Psalm 2. To prove his point that Jesus has a name far greater than the angels, the author quotes verse seven of David's psalm. "You are my Son; today I have become your Father," the Father in heaven is quoted as saying to his Son. From all eternity Jesus is God's Son, second Person of the Triune God, true God with the Father and the Holy Ghost.

But that name "Son" is his also in a special sense. The angel Gabriel referred to it in Luke 1:32 when he told Mary of that child to be born of her, "He will be great and will be called the Son of the Most High." In his incarnation Jesus inherited the name "Son" also according to his human nature. The God-man Jesus is God's Son. At the Jordan where Jesus was baptized and on the Mount of Transfiguration where his glory shone, the Father said it for all to hear, "You are my Son, whom I love" (Luke 3:22, 9:35).

With the resurrection the Father placed the exclamation point behind that statement. Read Acts 13:33 to see how Paul used this very verse from Psalm 2 and connected it with Christ's resurrection to show that Jesus was the Son of God. The word "today" refers to the whole matter of the Son becoming man to take away the world's sins, the mission on which the Father had sent him and which marked him far superior to the angels.

Next follows 2 Samuel 7:14: "I will be his father and he will be my son." Spoken originally about Solomon, these words had deeper meaning. They pointed ahead to David's greater Son, the eternal one whose kingdom would never end. Note how the author doubles the words. It is not enough to call Jesus "Son"; he also calls God "Father." Never was such divine sonship claimed for the angels.

Do we need more proof that Jesus is superior to the angels? Then look ahead to that great day of judgment when God will again "bring his first-born into the world." On that day Christ will surely stand out as "first-born," first in rank and position, as all the angels — not just some here and some there — but all the angels bow down before him in worship. In Revelation 5:11,12 John gives us a preview of the scene: "Then I looked and heard the voice of many angels, numbering thousands upon thousands, and ten thousand times ten thousand. . . . In a loud voice they sang: 'Worthy is the Lamb, who was slain, to receive power and wealth and wisdom and strength and honor and glory and praise!' "

Some are troubled by the last part of verse six. In the Hebrew text the words, "Let all God's angels worship him," are missing from Deuteronomy 32:43. Those words, however, are found in the Septuagint, the ancient Greek translation of the Old Testament, which the author of Hebrews evidently uses here. This seeming problem will not trouble us when we remember that the author of Hebrews quotes as guided by the Holy Spirit. The Spirit himself interprets, guiding his New Testament author to see the intent and meaning of the Old Testament prophet.

7In speaking of the angels he says, "He makes his angels winds, his servants flames of fire." 8But about the Son he says, "Your throne, O God, will last forever and ever, and righteousness will be the scepter of your kingdom. 9You have loved righteousness and hated wickedness; therefore God, your God, has set you above your companions by anointing you with the oil of joy." 10He also says, "In the beginning, O Lord, you laid the foundations of the earth, and the heavens are the work of your hands. 11They will perish, but you remain; they will all wear out like a garment. 12You will roll them up like a robe; like a garment they will be

changed. But you remain the same, and your years will never end." ¹³To which of the angels did God ever say, "Sit at my right hand until I make your enemies a footstool for your feet"? ¹⁴Are not all angels ministering spirits sent to serve those who will inherit salvation?

Superior in name, the Son is also superior in nature. Quoting Psalm 104:4 the author speaks of "angels," which means "messengers," and of "servants," a word which referred to people functioning in an office. True, the angels are exalted messengers and function in high capacity. Fleet as the wind, they carried God's messages to some; ferocious as fire, they executed his judgments on others. Through the angel Mary heard God's message in Luke 1:26-38, and through an angel King Herod felt God's judgment in Acts 12:23. But that's all the angels can be — messengers and servants under God's complete control.

Now look at Psalm 45:6,7 and see the supremacy of the Son. "O God," both the Psalmist and the author of Hebrews call him, God whose "throne will last for ever and ever." He's no mere messenger, but the eternal ruler of all. And a perfect ruler! His scepter is "righteousness." There is no partiality or prejudice with him, as with earthly kings; but a ruling that is straightforward and right. In his heart is love for righteousness and hatred for wickedness as evidenced during his life on earth. During those 33 years there was no flaw or failure, but perfect doing of his Father's will. Now "anointed with the oil of joy," a reference to the perfect joy and bliss at God's right hand, the ascended God-man rules in heaven. The Father, overjoyed at the completion and completeness of his Son's work, has set him far above his "companions," those believers who will share his gladness.

There is still more. Look at the splendid sunsets, the splashing ocean, the star-studded sky. The Son was there before they existed! He even helped lay their foundations.

Those foundations, seemingly so solid, will wear out like clothing and will be rolled up to be discarded and replaced. "But you," the author quotes Psalm 102:25-27 as referring to Jesus, "you remain the same, your years will never end." Age cannot touch him; death cannot breathe upon him; his years never come to an end. This eternal, unchangeable King is truly "Jesus Christ, the same yesterday, and today, and forever." What a ruler he is! His throne starts in a stable; his scepter is held in sinless hands; his kingdom lasts forever; his brothers share his glad joy.

The author concludes with the telling words of Psalm 110:1. No angel ever heard God say, "Sit at my right hand." That position of power and glory is reserved for the Son. All his enemies lie helpless in the dust before him as a footstool beneath his feet. All of history becomes *his*-story, which he writes in the eternal interest of his church.

And the angels? The best they can do is to be "ministering spirits sent to serve those who will inherit salvation." To carry out God's will for the believers is their task and also their limit. All the journey home even the lowliest believer can have their service, but far better to have him who is in every way "superior to the angels," the eternal Savior who promises in 13:5, "Never will I leave you; never will I forsake you."

WARNING:
DO NOT DRIFT AWAY FROM WHAT YOU HAVE HEARD

2 **We must pay more careful attention, therefore, to what we have heard, so that we do not drift away. ²For if the message spoken by angels was binding, and every violation and disobedience received its just punishment, ³how shall we escape if we ignore such a great salvation? This salvation, which was first announced by the Lord, was confirmed to us by those who heard him. ⁴God also testified to it by signs, wonders and various miracles, and gifts of the Holy Spirit distributed according to his will.**

How much like a pastor the author was. In the midst of documenting the supremacy of Christ as the final revelation of God and one far superior to the angels, he stops in pastoral concern to warn his readers. "We must pay more careful attention, therefore, to what we have heard," he tells them, "so that we do not drift away." Both terms take us down to the sea. "Drift away" reminds us of a ship that is drifting past, instead of into the safety of the harbor. Some wayward wind is carrying it slowly, almost unnoticed, past its destination. "Pay more careful attention" reminds us of sailors sweating and straining, sparing no effort to bring their ship safely to the dock.

This was no idle concern on the part of the author. The drifting past the harbor had already begun for those Jewish Christians. The winds of persecution and oppression were carrying them farther out to sea. Someone had to shout out to them, to warn them to head back into port. Then, as now, drifting away from God and his word can be such a slow, unnoticed process. Like some tire with a leaky valve, faith can lose its air little by little till it is completely flat.

So the author warned them strongly, reinforcing his warning with a searching question. All of those Jewish readers knew how serious God's law was. Even the giving of the law showed its seriousness. God himself spoke it (Exodus 20:1), writing it on two tablets of stone (Deuteronomy 5:22), using ANGELS in some way to transmit it (Galatians 3:19), and binding everyone to it. Everyone who violated the law by stepping over it in thought, word, or deed and everyone who disobeyed it by being unwilling to hear it would be justly punished. No sin of commission or omission would go unpunished by a fair and impartial God; so the Old Testament history of God's people plainly showed.

If that was how God felt about the law, the author argues going from the lesser to the greater, then "how shall we

15

escape if we ignore such a great salvation?" How great that salvation was he goes on to detail. It was "first announced by the Lord." Not angels, but the Lord himself brought the glorious gospel message. It was he who said in Luke 19:10, "The Son of Man came to seek and to save what was lost." From his own lips came those words in Matthew 20:28, "The Son of Man (came) . . . to give his life a ransom for many." He himself is both messenger and message, both proclaiming the good news and making it possible by the sacrifice of himself.

Nor did the proclamation of this great salvation cease with his ascension. Commissioned by him, the first disciples went about their task of witnessing and confirming what they had heard firsthand. "Confirm" is a legal term designating something properly documented. What court in the land will throw out evidence brought by actual eyewitnesses?

Nor did God leave those apostles to bear witness alone. He "also testified to it by signs, wonders and various miracles, and gifts of the Holy Spirit distributed according to his will." The gospel was not human speculation, but divine revelation. It was not man's thoughts, but God's truth. And God plainly showed this!

"Signs" puts the stress on the meaning of the miracles. The miracles were not to be pointless displays, but pointers — just as when Jesus in John 6 fed 5,000 and then used this miracle as a sign to point to himself as the Bread of Life.

"Wonders" refers to the effect of the miracle on the observers, and "miracles" refers to the superhuman power involved pointing to the Omnipotent as the source.

The Holy Spirit distributed his gifts in order to authenticate the gospel message. Let those who today insist upon such gifts mark well those words, "According to his will." The Spirit gave what, to whom, when, and where he willed. And when he gave, it was to testify to that great message of salvation.

Such was the message, given by God himself, confirmed by those who heard it, authenticated by the gifts of the Spirit. This is the only message that can save. To both believer and unbeliever goes that serious question, "How shall we escape if we ignore such a great salvation?" The author leaves the question hanging hauntingly in the air. Let each one answer for himself. And let each one heed the author's advice, "We must pay more attention to what we have heard."

⁵It is not to angels that he has subjected the world to come, about which we are speaking. ⁶But there is a place where someone has testified: "What is man that you are mindful of him, the son of man that you care for him? ⁷You made him a little lower than the angels; you crowned him with glory and honor ⁸and put everything under his feet." In putting everything under him, God left nothing that is not subject to him. Yet as present we do not see everything subject to him. ⁹But we see Jesus, who was made a little lower than the angels, now crowned with glory and honor because he suffered death, so that by the grace of God he might taste death for everyone.

In 1:14 the author has described the believers as heirs of salvation. Now with his pastoral warning done, he again takes up that thought. He is writing not about this little earth which man inhabits for only a few years and where he can claim lasting title to no more than a burial plot, but about "the world to come." In that promised land of heaven, not the angels, but man will rule with Christ. Believers will sit on the throne with him who is the "heir of all things." Just what this world to come and our kingship there involve, Scripture does not fully tell us, but it does clearly tell us how to get there.

How insignificant mankind appears, just some speck, when contrasted to the starry heavens. But look what God has made of him! Quoting from Psalm 8 the author marvels along with David at God's gracious dealings with mankind.

First God made man an object of his special favor. He who orders the universe and holds the heavens in his hands is concerned about and cares for man. He remembers man constantly and looks in on him and cares for him in hundreds of ways.

Next, God made man a creature of special privilege, not classed with the animals, but far above the rest of creation, and just a little lower than the exalted angels. There was even more. God made man a creature of unique dignity and unrivaled dominion. Glory and honor were due him as the crowning part of God's creation. To show this, God "put everything under his feet." And that means what it says as the author shows by emphasizing, "God left nothing that is not subject to him."

Doesn't that sound like an echo of Genesis 1:26-28 where "God said, 'Let us make man in our image, in our likeness, and let them rule over the fish of the sea and the birds of the air, over the livestock, over all the earth, and over all the creatures that move along the ground.' So God created man in his own image, in the image of God he created him; male and female he created them"? Yes, what is man that God should so graciously deal with him?

Yet is that what we see when we look at mankind today? He who was made for dominion is now often dominated. He who was to rule has let his scepter slip. The author needed not explain how man came to abuse his privileges, ignore his destiny, and be limited in his dominion. The readers would know about the events in the Garden of Eden, how sin had turned man from victor into victim. Thus it came about that "at present we do not see everything subject to him."

But even now we do see Jesus crowned with glory and honor. The author uses the human name "Jesus" to remind us of how God became a man like us. Our Lord did not sit in some remote throne room in heaven, watching and sadly shaking his head at our feeble, futile efforts. Instead, he himself came down to earth and took on our human nature. What a sight that must have been for the angels as their Lord stepped down from his eternal glory to be wrapped in human flesh and made a little lower than they.

But now he is "crowned with honor and glory" in a higher sense than David meant when he spoke of man in Psalm 8. His is "the name that is above every name," a name at which "every knee should bow, in heaven and on earth and under the earth, and every tongue confess that Jesus Christ is Lord, to the glory of God the Father," as Philippians 2:9-11 relates.

All this "because he suffered death, so that by the grace of God he might taste death for everyone." Jesus became man to die for man. "To taste death" is more than merely to sip at that dread cup. It is to drain it completely, to experience it fully. And this he did "for everyone," the author writes, using the singular so that all can say, "He died for *me.*" Also the author reminds us that he did this "by the grace of God." "Grace" is one of those great Christian words and refers to a gift which is completely undeserved. Certainly that word belongs here, for it is God's undeserved gift that Jesus tasted death fully for all guilty sinners and in this way paid for their sins.

How can man reach the promised land? How can he be prepared to live and reign in the world to come? There is only one way — by seeing Jesus. Only through Jesus' saving work can man's glorious destiny become eternal reality. From such a Jesus who would dare turn away?

10In bringing many sons to glory, it was fitting that God, for whom and through whom everything exists, should make the author of their salvation perfect through suffering. 11Both the one who makes men holy and those who are made holy are of the same family. So Jesus is not ashamed to call them brothers. 12He says,

"I will declare your name to my brothers; in the presence of the congregation I will sing your praises." [13]And again, "I will put my trust in him." And again he says, "Here am I, and the children God has given me."

Might there be objection to man's being raised to glory through Jesus' suffering? Then let it be known that this plan of salvation was no haphazard happening. It began in the heart and the mind of an eternal God "for whom and through whom everything exists." God, for whose glory and by whose hand all exists, allows nothing — certainly not the plan of salvation — to occur by accident.

A just and holy God did not bring men to heaven's glory by ignoring their sins, but rather by dealing with them. This he did by sending his Son to be the "author of their salvation." "Author" can also be translated as "source" and would then parallel the thought in 5:9 where we read, "He (Christ) became the source of eternal salvation for all who obey him." Jesus didn't merely lead to salvation. He did more than blaze a trail to heaven; he became the Way without which, as John 14:6 asserts, "no one comes to the Father."

When the author said of this source of salvation that God "made him perfect through suffering," he used a word that meant to "reach a goal." Jesus' goal was to prepare salvation and this he did through his suffering. Without his suffering death, none would be brought to glory as God's sons. Such was the plan that came from God's eternal heart of love.

What love that had to be, one which caused the Lord of all to stoop down to earth and become one with man. Both he who makes men holy and those who are made holy are of the same family, sharing the same Father and the same human nature, though Jesus was without sin. They are truly brothers and Jesus did not shrink from declaring the fact.

Again the author turns to the Old Testament to quote convincingly for his Jewish readers. Fittingly in a section speaking of Christ's suffering, he turns to Psalm 22, a messianic psalm which foretold Jesus' death. That suffering Savior would faithfully declare his Father's name to his brothers. Not only did he show them what his Father was like; he also joined them in singing psalms and praises to him.

Next the author brings two quotations from Isaiah chapter 8. In verse 17, speaking as a type of the Messiah, the prophet said, "I will put my trust in him." Look at Christ's life on earth, listen to his prayers, and note his complete dependence on God. Even when dying, it was, "Father, into your hands I commit my spirit" (Luke 23:46). Then in verse 18 it was, "Here am I, and the children God has given me."

Though like Isaiah the Messiah had his message rejected and was himself oppressed by those around him, yet along with the children, the believers God had given him, he trusted in his Father. All three quotations locate Christ firmly among those he came to save. All three cause us to marvel at a love that would make Christ our brother.

14Since the children have flesh and blood, he too shared in their humanity so that by his death he might destroy him who holds the power of death — that is, the devil — 15and free those who all their lives were held in slavery by their fear of death. 16For surely it is not angels he helps, but Abraham's descendants. 17For this reason he had to be made like his brothers in every way, in order that he might become a merciful and faithful high priest in service to God, and that he might make atonement for the sins of the people. 18Because he himself suffered when he was tempted, he is able to help those who are being tempted.

What did Christ accomplish by becoming our brother? The author points us first of all to Satan. "Destroy" is not to wipe out, but to nullify or render ineffective. That's what

21

Christ did to the devil, the one "who holds the power of death." Death was the hold the devil had over man. Only God controls death absolutely, determining who is to die and when. But in bringing sin into the world, the devil brought death on earth and in hell as sin's wage. As long as he can keep man sinning, he can demand that this horrible wage be paid. And the result for the sinner? Lifelong slavery spent cringing in fear as Satan cracks death's whip.

But no more! Instead, the believer joins Paul in the fearless declaration of Philippians 1:23, "I desire to depart and be with Christ which is better by far." Jesus, our brother, has nullified the devil and neutralized his ultimate weapon of death. To accomplish this he "shared in our inheritance." He took on our flesh and blood that he might die and with his holy death free us from our bondage. Jesus used that very thing with which Satan was bullying and battering man to defeat Satan. Like some vicious dog Satan has been chained, and if some still die of his rabid bite, it is because they have strayed too close to him and too far away from the Prince of Life.

What else did Christ accomplish? Using terminology his readers as "Abraham's descendants" could well understand, the author described Christ as "a merciful and faithful high priest in service to God." Only in the book of Hebrews is Jesus called "high priest," and what a high priest he was. Toward his brethren he was merciful, feeling their needs and rising to meet them fully. Toward God he was faithful in service, omitting nothing, but carrying out his Father's will in unswerving obedience even when it meant suffering and death.

"Atonement" was another word well known to Jewish readers. It took them back to the Old Testament, to that great day of Atonement, when the high priest entered be-

22

hind the curtain in the temple to sprinkle the animal blood on the mercy seat. In this way sin's removal and the resulting peace with God were symbolized.

Now look at our high priest! The blood he sprinkles is his own. It's not just symbolic, but holy, precious blood, powerful enough to remove sin's deepest stain and to effect true atonement by satisfying God's wrath over sin forever. Such help he brought not for sinless and deathless angels, but for sinful and mortal man.

With "Abraham's descendants" and "the people" the author was referring to Israel since his readers were Jewish and descendants of those to whom the ancient promise of salvation had been given. This does not deny the fact that Christ paid also for the sins of the Gentiles. For if Israel needed such a high priest, so does all the rest of mankind.

One additional point the author mentions, this one also resting on Jesus' incarnation. The untempted can have no compassion, the conquered can lend no assistance, but the tempted and triumphant God-man surely can. It was indeed fitting that God should bring Jesus to his goal through suffering (2:10). Though his temptations were different from ours in that they came entirely from without and never from within, yet they were very real. The sight of him writhing in Gethsemane's dust reminds us just how real they were. But he conquered! Now our temptations are his special concern and he stands ready to champion us against every assault. Not only those beleaguered Jewish Christians needed that assurance, so do we.

Christ Is Superior to Moses

3 **Therefore, holy brothers, who share in the heavenly calling, fix your thoughts on Jesus, the apostle and high priest whom**

we confess. [2]He was faithful to the one who appointed him, just as Moses was faithful in all God's house. [3]Jesus has been found worthy of greater honor than Moses, just as the builder of a house has greater honor than the house itself. [4]For every house is built by someone, but God is the builder of everything. [5]Moses was faithful as a servant in all God's house, testifying to what would be said in the future. [6]But Christ is faithful as a son over God's house. And we are his house, if we hold on to our courage and the hope of which we boast.

Steadily the author has been advancing the argument that Jesus is superior to anyone and anything. Now he turns to an Old Testament figure most significant in Jewish history and thought. It was very difficult for a Jew to think of anyone greater than Moses. Even the New Testament refers to Moses' greatness, mentioning him some 80 times, more often than any other Old Testament figure. But great as Moses was, Jesus was far greater. As a result, to forsake Jesus would bring results far more terrible than to forsake Moses. What a warning for those Jewish readers being tempted by persecution to do just that.

"Holy brothers, who share in the heavenly calling," the author began his earnest warning. For the first time in the letter he addressed his readers, making his admonition all the more warm and vital. "Brothers" they were, fellow believers in Christ, "holy," cleansed from sin and consecrated for service by Jesus the high priest. Theirs was a "heavenly calling" both coming from and ultimately leading to God in heaven. Such a calling they surely would not want to jeopardize.

So the author warns them, "Fix your thoughts on Jesus." Serious attention was necessary; careful, constant study of Jesus. The use of the personal name immediately focuses attention on his work on earth, the mission God became

Moses with the Ten Commandments

man in order to fulfill. The joint title "the apostle and high priest" also focuses on that work. "Apostle," used only here of Jesus in the New Testament, involves the thought of mission, referring to one who is commissioned for something. God had sent his Son as the authorized envoy to speak for him and carry out his will. "High priest" refers to the sacrificial nature of his mission as we have previously noted in 2:17 and will see again later in greater detail. Such was the Jesus those readers already had confessed and still needed to confess as the sum and substance of their faith.

Jesus' superiority to Moses was not a matter of faithfulness. Both were faithful in carrying out their assigned tasks. In Numbers 12:7 God himself said of Moses, "He is faithful in all my house." Moses poured out his life in service to the house of Israel, God's chosen Old Testament people. He even offered to have his name blotted out of God's book in exchange for them. Nor can anyone doubt Jesus' faithfulness to the one who had commissioned him apostle and high priest. In John 17:4 on Maundy Thursday evening he could say to his Father, "I have brought you glory on earth by completing the work you gave me to do."

The point of comparison was not faithfulness, but position. No one would give to any house, no matter how grandiosely built and furnished, more honor than that given to the builder. To rank both builder and building on the same level is foolish. Now look at Moses and Jesus. Though important as their leader, Moses was only part of the house of Israel. Jesus as God was the builder of that house, just as he is the "builder of everything." As a creature Moses occupied a high position in Israel and was worthy of honor. As the Creator of all, including Moses and Israel, Jesus was worthy of the highest honor.

Just as the creator is superior to the creature, so is the son to the servant. Moses was a "servant" in the house of Israel, a term which refers not to some slave who serves because he has to, but to a free servant who serves because he wants to. He was a faithful servant as shown by the refrain running through Exodus, "According to all the Lord commanded, so did he." His greatest service was "testifying to what would be said in the future." In John 5:46 Jesus explained what this meant when he told the Jews of his day, "If you believed Moses, you would believe me, for he wrote about me."

But "Christ" is greater, the author declares, using this title for the first time so far in the book. "Christ" marks his high office and the honor due him, for he was not servant in the house, but "Son over God's house." He owns the house, building it and ruling over it. And this "house" is not off in the distant future, as was the case in Moses' time, but the author speaks of it as a present reality. To which house does the author refer with the words, "We are his house"? It is the one described in Ephesians 2:20,21 as the "household built on the foundation of the apostles and prophets, with Christ Jesus himself as the chief cornerstone. In him the whole building is joined together and rises to become a holy temple in the Lord." All believers of Old and New Testaments are part of this glorious house, built on and ruled by the Son.

Watch out, though! Some have lost their place in this glorious house as the author will show directly. In our verse, however, he offers encouragement, urging us to "hold on to our courage and the hope of which we boast." "Courage" is that feeling of confidence which allows words to flow freely. Such subjective courage is nothing without the objective "hope of which we boast." The word for "boast" refers to the cause for boasting, not to the act. "Hope" points out the cause and content of our boasting, lifting our eyes of faith to what we have and ever will have in that superior Christ Jesus!

WARNING:

DO NOT HARDEN YOUR HEARTS IN UNBELIEF AS DID ISRAEL

[7]So, as the Holy Spirit says: "Today, if you hear his voice, [8]do not harden your hearts as you did in the rebellion, during the time of testing in the desert, [9]where your fathers tested and tried me and for forty years saw what I did. [10]That is why I was angry with that generation, and I said, 'Their hearts are always going astray, and they have not known my ways.' [11]So I declared on oath in my anger, 'They shall never enter my rest.' "

From a comparison between Christ and Moses the author turns to one between their followers. For Jewish readers there could be no more effective warning example than what happened to Israel during its forty years of wilderness wandering. Moses recorded those events particularly on the pages of Exodus, and David summarized them anew in Psalm 95:7-11. Now quoting from David's psalm, the author states, "The Holy Spirit says." Again we have the fact of inspiration. David's words are the Spirit's words. Later in 4:7 this same verse is repeated and the author states even more specifically, "He (God) spoke through David."

What does God have to say to us through David? Something extremely serious: "Today, if you hear his voice, do not harden your hearts." "Today" is the present, the time when God speaks, a day whose length he alone determines. To "harden" contains the picture of something dried and stiff, like the branch of a tree that will not bend or yield. Applied to the heart, which the Jew viewed as the seat of his entire being, it meant spiritual catastrophe. It described a heart which knew better, one which had tasted and knew the blessings of God, but which in deliberate unbelief then turned away from those blessings. Such a phenomenon might be called spiritual suicide since it is impossible for the Spirit to work repentance in such hearts while they cling to deliberate unbelief.

Look at Israel in the wilderness! Of the 600,000 men over 20 years old standing victoriously on the shores of the Red Sea at the beginning of the Exodus, only Joshua and Caleb finally entered the promised land. Because of their hardened hearts the others filled grave after grave dotting the wilderness trail. In the Hebrew of Psalm 95 "rebellion" and "testing" are the proper nouns "Meribah" and "Massah." They refer to the events at Rephidim, where the people grumbled because they had no water to drink (Exodus 17). In the Septuagint, the Greek translation of the Old Testament, from which the author quotes, they are rendered "rebellion" and "testing" and are used here to refer to the whole forty-year period. From beginning to end, for forty years, like some river gradually freezing over in the winter, the hardening process went on. Though they saw what God did for them, how he never once let them down, yet in stubborn unbelief they kept on testing and trying him. Their eyes saw, but their hearts did not, instead insisting always on new evidence of God's presence in their midst.

Following the thoughts of Psalm 95, the author of *Hebrews* quotes God as saying, "That is why I was angry with that generation." "Angry" is a strong word and shows God's inevitable reaction to sin. The holy God, described in 12:29 as a "consuming fire," does not treat sin lightly nor forever put up with the sinner. Where hearts go astray by completely ignoring his "today" and constantly spurning his "ways," another reaction comes, as Israel discovered. Having exhausted God's grace in the wilderness, Israel heard God swear in righteous anger, "They shall never enter my rest."

When God swears, it is always irrevocable and always serious. To lose the earthly Canaan was serious enough, but it was far more serious to lose the heavenly one. The warning for all readers is clear — do not repeat the mistakes of those Israelites!

[12]See to it, brothers, that none of you has a sinful, unbelieving heart that turns away from the living God. [13]But encourage one another daily, as long as it is called Today, so that none of you may be hardened by sin's deceitfulness. [14]We have come to share in Christ if we hold firmly till the end of the confidence we had at first.

With pastoral concern the author now applies this warning to his readers and fellow believers. "See to it that none of you has a sinful, unbelieving heart," he urges, wanting not a single one of them to be lost. Unbelief is always a heart problem, one that deals with the inner being. And unbelief is always serious because it rejects Christ's salvation.

The unbelieving heart against which the author warns each of his readers is one "that turns away from the living God." It is not a matter of casual drifting but of deliberate desertion by hearts which once heard and believed, but then cut themselves off from the living God. Were any of the readers inclined because of persecution's heat to rebel against Jesus by turning back to Judaism? Let them be warned! To turn away from Jesus is to reject the living God. In John 5:23 Jesus said, "He who does not honor the Son does not honor the Father, who sent him."

All of them needed constant encouragement from one another. Sin can be so violently deceitful. It disguises its horrible purpose, dilutes its poisonous taste and in the end utterly destroys. Did the sin of turning from Christ back to Judaism seem not so serious, perhaps even prudent in the face of persecution? "Watch out," the author warns, "that is sin's deceitful course and can lead to hardened hearts." "Help each other watch out," the author also urges, reminding his readers that no believer exists as an island. Christian faith and spiritual health are not just matters between a man and his God. They are of vital concern among fellow believers. Gathering together in local congregations is more than advisable; it is necessary so that we can "encourage one another daily."

Believers share so much in Christ and have so much more waiting for them. All that the heaven-sent Savior offers is ours "if we hold firmly till the end the confidence we had at first." What a firm, confident stand those readers had when first brought to faith. How sad if any were now to turn out like the rocky soil of Mark 4:16,17, where the seed of faith "last[s] only a short time. When trouble or persecution comes because of the word, they quickly fall away."

15As it has just been said, "Today, if you hear his voice, do not harden your hearts as you did in the rebellion." 16Who were they who heard and rebelled? Were they not all those Moses led out of Egypt? 17And with whom was he angry for forty years? Was it not with those who sinned, whose bodies fell in the desert? 18And to whom did God swear that they would never enter his rest if not to those who disobeyed? 19So we see that they were not able to enter, because of their unbelief.

Once more the author warns his readers about hardening their hearts. With a series of hard-hitting questions he drives home his point. "Who were they who heard and rebelled?" Not people who were ignorant or had never experienced God's wonderous works and ways, but "all those Moses led out of Egypt." "With whom was he angry for forty years?" Not with those who didn't know any better or were innocent, but "those who sinned." God's anger is not capricious or hasty.

Forty years of rejection and rebellion by those who had richly experienced divine providence was the cause of all those graves dotting the desert. "And to whom did God swear that they would never enter his rest?" To people who had no excuse whatsoever, to those who knew better and yet disobeyed, refusing to believe. Can any reader miss the point? "So we see," the author concludes, "that they were not able to enter, because of their unbelief." What robbed that generation of Israel of rest both in the earthly and the heavenly Canaans? The answer is, "Unbelief." Will the consequences be any less severe for those who would turn away from the superior Jesus today?

So much seems to be demanded of those first readers and of us today. The race of faith is to be all out all the time; the course on which it is run is hazardous and obstacle filled; and it never lets up! How can we do it? How can we hold out? "Fix your thoughts on Jesus," the author urges, "the apostle and high priest whom we confess." Let that superior Jesus and his Word be the sure basis of our confidence. God rest our faith not on what we are, but on what Jesus is: not on what we do, but on what Jesus has done. Then our journey in life's wilderness, unlike Israel's, will have both a good beginning and a good end.

BUT SEEK THE REST THEY LOST

4 **Therefore, since the promise of entering his rest still stands, let us be careful that none of you be found to have fallen short of it. ²For we also have had the gospel preached to us, just as they did; but the message they heard was of no value to them, because those who heard did not combine it with faith. ³Now we who have believed enter that rest, just as God has said, "So I declared on oath in my anger, they shall never enter my rest." And yet his work has**

been finished since the creation of the world. ⁴For somewhere he has spoken about the seventh day in these words, "And on the seventh day God rested from all his work." ⁵And again in the passage above he says, "They shall never enter my rest."

The key word in this section is "rest." Eight times the author uses it, in addition to the special word "Sabbath-rest." That rest of which he writes must be important. The eternal rest awaiting all believers in Christ in heaven is all-important, so that the author's pastoral heart reaches out in urgent warning to his readers. "Let us be careful," he urges, "that none of you be found to have fallen short of it." He wanted not a single one of them to miss out on the heavenly rest into which God himself entered when he had finished his work of creation and to which the entry of Israel into Canaan under Joshua pointed.

But that rest is not reached automatically. Unbelieving Israel in the wilderness stood as a warning example of how that rest could be lost. Let those who still have the "promise" — a word which the author uses fourteen times, more than any other New Testament book — be on their guard. If Israel with all their advantages lost the promised rest, so might the readers. "Let us be careful," the author therefore urged, "that none of you be found to have fallen short of it."

How did Israel and how might the readers lose this heavenly rest? It was not because they had not heard about it or did not know how to enter it. "We also have had the gospel preached to us, just as they did," the author reminded them. Entrance into God's eternal rest through the promised Savior was no mystery concealed from them. "Your father Abraham rejoiced at the thought of seeing my day; he saw it and was glad," Jesus could tell the Jews in John 8:56, and in 5:46, referring to Moses, who had led them in the wilderness, Jesus could say, "He wrote about me."

The Old Testament people, including the Jews of the Exodus, had this gospel promise in prophecy; the Hebrew Christians, to whom the author was writing, had it in fulfillment. Both looked to the same key to open the door to heaven's rest, the Savior on the cross of Calvary. Old Testament believers looked ahead to him while New Testament believers look back. It is the same Savior for all.

"But," the author warns, "the message they heard was of no value to [did not benefit] them, because those who heard did not combine it with faith [did not share in the faith]." Did those Hebrew Christians, tempted to forsake Christ, get the warning? Do we? Faith is not a matter of the ears only, but of the heart. The gospel message, when it beats on the eardrums only, leads to no eternal rest. *Faith* is required, the author reminds us, using for the first time this word which is also a favorite of his. Israel lost the promised rest because of the lack of faith. Must not our constant prayer as we hear that precious gospel be, "I do believe, help me overcome my unbelief!" (Mark 9:24)?

For unbelievers there is no heavenly rest, but for believers it is sure and certain. "We who have believed enter that rest," the author writes, using the present tense. Entering that rest is going on right now. "I tell you the truth, whoever hears my word and believes him who sent me HAS eternal life and will not be condemned; he *HAS CROSSED OVER* from death to life," Jesus said in John 5:24. We "*HAVE TASTED* the goodness of the word of God and the powers of the coming age," the author himself writes in 6:5. Both quotations point to our present entering of that rest.

Yes, we are but strangers here and heaven is our home. Step by step we walk the wilderness trail to that home and the perfect rest it offers. But even while on the road, as long as the journey takes, that rest is ours. The sip we have of that perfect peace and complete fellowship with God makes us long to drain the whole cup of that which God simply calls "my rest." Where do we find the ability to fathom or the words to describe fully what all is contained in that phrase, "my rest"?

Again the author quotes Psalm 95:11. When God in righteous anger swore that Israel in the wilderness would not enter his rest, he was not tearing up his promise or nailing two-by-fours across heaven's door. That joyous rest is still there, just as it always has been and ever will be. This important truth the author reinforces by taking us back to the creation of the world.

In three different places (Genesis 2:2, Exodus 20:11, 31:17), so that the author says "somewhere," the Old Testament stated, "On the seventh day God rested from all his work." Note the fact of inspiration again. Though Moses wrote those verses, yet the author states, "He (God) has spoken about the seventh day." What was that rest of God on the seventh day? It certainly could not have been weariness as if six days of calling all into being had tired him out. In 40:28 Isaiah reminds us, "The Lord is the everlasting God, the Creator of the ends of the earth. He will not grow tired or weary." Nor was it inactivity as if he stopped watching over the sparrows or counting the hairs on our heads. In John 5:17 Jesus told the Jews, "My Father is always at his work to this very day, and I, too, am working."

God's rest on the seventh day was the rest that follows finished and holy work, a rest characterized by perfect contentment and infinite satisfaction. It is this rest, this eternal blessedness and total fulfillment, that he wants to share with his children. When we read Genesis chapter one, we notice that each day of creation is described the same way, "There was evening and there was morning." But of the seventh day this is not said. Each of those six days of creation had an ending as well as a beginning, but of the day of rest this is not stated. Of course, that seventh day also had to be a twenty-four hour day as the others, but the rest it symbolized has no ending.

Ever since creation ended and in spite of man's sin, God's rest is open. "*They* shall never enter my rest," God said of Israel, but others will. To a world wearing itself out under sin's load and wearied by sin's consequences, the eternal God stretches out hands in open invitation, "Come to me ... and I will give you rest" (Matthew 11:28). The beauty of it is that he not only invites, but his grace through word and sacrament produces in us the faith necessary for entrance into that eternal rest.

⁶It still remains that some will enter that rest, and those who formerly had the gospel preached to them did not go in, because of their disobedience. ⁷Therefore God again set a certain day, calling it Today, when a long time later he spoke through David, as was said before, "Today, if you hear his voice, do not harden your hearts." ⁸For if Joshua had given them rest, God would not have spoken later about another day. ⁹There remains, then, a Sabbath-rest for the people of God; ¹⁰for anyone who enters God's rest also rests from his own work, just as God did from his. ¹¹Let us, therefore, make every effort to enter that rest, so that no one will fall by following their example of disobedience.

In 40:8 of his book Isaiah declared, "The word of our God stands forever," and in Matthew 24:35 Jesus repeated the thought, "My words will never pass away." God's word is always sure. He promised rest; his promise still stands even though Israel lost the rest; his promise will be fulfilled in others entering that rest. "Some will enter that rest," the text says, reminding us with "some" that God wants as many as possible. Again we note that the way into his rest is through "the gospel preached" to men and that there is a close connection between the gospel and faith. Israel in the wilderness lost the rest "because of their disobedience," a word always used in the New Testament for disobeying God. Often that word is used in connection with the gospel and means as much as unbelief, the refusal to believe God's promises.

But the "today" in which God offered his rest did not end with the sad incident in the desert. "A long time later," over 400 years in fact, we hear him offering his rest to the Israel of David's time. Nor did his "today" end with them. To Hebrew Christians reading his words centuries later, to all who read them today, he still speaks. The present is God's "today" for us. Only he knows how long it will last. Through the word his voice speaks to us proclaiming the gospel and offering his rest in more glorious form than Israel ever heard it.

The reference to Joshua in verse eight reinforces the proper identification of the rest of which God speaks. This was no mere entrance into an earthly land of Canaan such as Joshua effected for the children of that wayward generation of Israelites. It's the heavenly Canaan, as God's speaking of it through David hundreds of years later plainly showed. In the Greek the names Joshua and Jesus are the same; the context must help determine which one is meant. What a thought! The first "Joshua" could not lead them into God's true rest, but there was another one who could and did, with his life-blood as the price.

The point is clear — "there remains, then, a Sabbath-rest for the people of God." "Sabbath-rest," the author calls it, combining thoughts by using a term found only here in the New Testament. "The people of God," the spiritual Israel of all true believers, have the eternal Sabbath-rest of peace and pardon, union and communion with God, with its fulness to be reached in heaven. God's resting on that first Sabbath after creation typified this wondrous rest as did all the Sabbaths observed in the Old Testament.

For us in the New Testament the picture is even clearer. Those Sabbath days were, as Colossians 2:17 points out, "a shadow of the things that were to come; the reality, however, is found in Christ." In Christ, shadow has become reality. Through his death and resurrection the way to God's eternal rest is fully built and opened wide. What we need now are not Old Testament Sabbath days, but a faith in Christ "that will not shrink though pressed by many a foe."

Rest implies cessation from work, a laying down of that which tires. So also with the heavenly rest which Christ brings and to which he leads. "Anyone who enters God's rest also rests from his own work," the author reminds us. Before faith, man seeks to work out his own salvation. He sweats and strains futilely and fearfully, seeking to remove sin's stain and pay its penalty. What rest is his when by faith he hears the Lord's words as recorded in Isaiah 40:1,2, "Comfort, comfort my people . . . Speak tenderly to Jerusalem, and proclaim to her that her hard service has been completed, that her sin has been paid for, that she has received from the Lord's hand double for all her sins."

How quickly he who knows and trusts Christ's work will lay down the vain labors of his own hands. After salvation, the believer still labors. He spends himself in living service to the One who loved him and gave himself for him. Of that service we never grow weary, though we often weary in it. How wonderful when the time comes and we hear that voice from heaven as recorded in Revelation 14:13 saying, "Blessed are the dead who die in the Lord from now on. Yes, says the Spirit, they will rest from their labor, for their deeds will follow them."

Such glorious rest the believer tastes now in part and wants to taste in heaven fully and forever. That's why he listens carefully as the author with his pastoral heart full of concern warns, "Let us, therefore, make every effort to enter that rest." More is needed than a good beginning, more than nominal allegiance to the Christian flag, more than occasional lip-service to his word. Every effort must be expended if we are to reach that rest. Constant diligence must be given so that we do not end up like disobeying and disbelieving Israel in the desert. But that effort must be in the right direction, always closer to God's gospel through which his powerful grace works to shore up and strengthen weakening faith. Before we can pray, "Jesus, in mercy bring us to that dear land of rest," we need another prayer, the one that humbly asks, "Lord, open thou my heart to hear and through thy word to me draw near."

12The word of God is living and active. Sharper than any double-edged sword, it penetrates even to dividing soul and spirit, joints and marrow; it judges the thoughts and attitudes of the heart. 13Nothing in all creation is hidden from God's sight. Everything is uncovered and laid bare before the eyes of him to whom we must give account.

The author has forcefully set forth the fact that God grants his rest to believers, but denies it to unbelievers. Now he clearly reminds his readers that God's word can easily distinguish between the two. With "word of God" he refers not just to Psalm 95 or to the Old Testament, but also to all the New Testament Scriptures which those Jewish Christians had by that time. That word was no dry encyclopedia filled with dusty facts, no mere human word which is spoken and then quickly evaporates into the air. It has qualities which should make them sit up and pay attention to it as the author showed by setting forth three pairs of thoughts.

"The word of God is living and active," is the first pair. It is alive, filled with the vitality of God himself and therefore indestructible and imperishable. It is also "active." The word does things. It is not passive or outmoded, but always up-to-date and effective as God himself said in Isaiah 55:11, "It will not return to me empty, but will accomplish what I desire and achieve the purpose for which I sent it." The Samaritan woman at the well in John 4 and the thief on the cross to Jesus' right could tell us something about the life and energy of God's word.

It is "sharper than any double-edged sword; it penetrates even to dividing soul and spirit, joints and marrow," is the second pair. The short sword carried by the Roman legionary was sharp and with its double edge could cut in any direction. But God's word is far sharper and with its cutting edges can divide even the indivisible. It is difficult to make a distinction between "soul" and "spirit." They seem to be different functions of the same element, with "soul" referring more to man's lower physical life with its desires and interests and "spirit" referring more to his higher spiritual life with its need for fellowship with God. Who can tell where soul and spirit touch or divide? Yet God's word slices the two as easily as a sharp scissors glides through thin cloth. With "joints" and "marrow" the author advances a slightly different thought. God's word with its cutting edge lays bare the joints where the bones meet and even the bones themselves where the marrow lies. So deeply the word penetrates into man's innermost being, exposing his most secret parts. The people who heard Peter's sermon on Pentecost knew about the penetrating action of this double-edged sword. Acts 2:37

tells us, "When the people heard this, they were cut to the heart and said to Peter and the other apostles, 'Brothers, what shall we do?' "

The third pair says, "It judges the thoughts and attitudes of the heart. Nothing in all creation is hidden from God's sight. Everything is uncovered and laid bare before the eyes of him." The word of God is his eye to look into the hearts of men. With its piercing gaze it penetrates into the heart's deepest recesses and correctly judges the thoughts and attitudes it finds there. On the last day that word will also do the judging. In John 12:48 Jesus warned, "There is a judge for the one who rejects me and does not accept my words; that very word which I spoke will condemn him at the last day."

The same thought is expressed in the second half of this pair. By shifting from God's word to the person of God himself, the author shows how closely connected the two are. Under God's discerning gaze no one can hide himself or his deeds. "Everything is uncovered," that secret sin, that stowaway temptation, that little speck of decay, that slow shifting away from God and his word. Everything is "laid bare" before his eyes just as the neck of the sacrificial animal, bent to the side, lies completely exposed for the knife. So nothing and no one will be hidden from God's eyes.

Now comes the conclusion to which the author has been leading with the three pairs. He points to "him to whom we must give account." God's word brings life to us and eternity to our hearts. But if that word is neglected or spurned, the day will come when his word will compel us to look into his all-seeing eyes. To the unbeliever this thought is law, warning him that God cannot be fooled, neither will he be mocked. To the believer this thought is gospel, warming him with the thought that God knows all his weaknesses and stands ready to provide in Christ all that is needed. How vital for both is the recurring theme of this chapter, "Today, if you hear his voice, do not harden your hearts."

Christ Is Superior in His Priesthood
He Is a Priest Superior in Qualifications

[14]Therefore, since we have a great high priest who has gone through the heavens, Jesus, the Son of God, let us hold firmly to the faith we profess. [15]For we do not have a high priest who is unable to sympathize with our weaknesses, but we have one who has been tempted in every way, just as we are — yet was without sin. [16]Let us then approach the throne of grace with confidence, so that we may receive mercy and find grace to help us in our time of need.

"High priest" is a term which only the book of Hebrews applies to Jesus Christ. In fact, the thought of his high priesthood forms the central theme of this book. The author has been moving toward this important concept since the beginning of his book, as his hints in 2:17 and 3:1 have indicated. Now he leads us to closer contact with this theme, though we must wait till chapters 7, 8 and 9 for a fuller treatment.

The priesthood was basic to Judaism. Every Jew was familiar with the concept of the priests who officiated at the Jerusalem temple and of the high priest, who led them in their service. Did that Old Testament priesthood appeal to any of the readers? Was part of the argumentation for their backsliding from Christianity to Judaism the excuse that Christianity had no high priest? Then let them listen and learn. "We have a great high priest," the author writes. Never was it said of any Old Testament high priest that he was "great," not even of Aaron the first one. But of God's high priest it is said.

Moreover, this great high priest "has gone into heaven." Did his invisibility bother them? Did they prefer that visible priest from Aaron's line going on that annual Day of Atonement with the blood of the sacrifice across the temple courtyard into the Holy Place and then going where they could not see, beyond the veil into the Holy of Holies?

If so, let them remember that God's high priest has done more than pass through temple chambers like those earthly priests who are seen today and dead tomorrow. He has gone through the heavens to the throne of God, there to live and reign forever. His invisibility is his advantage; his absence indicates his greatness. The sacrifice he offered, the blood he carried to the mercy seat of God, was his own. He is "himself the Victim and himself the Priest." And his sacrifice was perfect. Only once did he have to bring it, not yearly like those high priests with the animal blood, as his ascension into heaven's glory well indicated.

Who is this "great high priest"? "Jesus the Son of God," the author clearly states, calling him "Jesus" to remind us of his humanity and "Son of God" to assure us of his divinity. Here is a high priest who is far superior to any earthly one because of his person and his work.

He is also our high priest! "We have a great high priest," the author reminded the Hebrews. God had given him to them. By God's grace they had professed Jesus and all that he offered as the substance of their faith. Now was no time to waver in that confession. Regardless what forces were pulling and pressing upon them, there was no room for cowardice. A great high priest who made life worth living and death worth dying dared not be lightly dismissed or thoughtlessly traded for something inferior. Instead, it was time to keep holding firmly to him and his blessings.

43

What about weaknesses? It's easy to say, "Let us hold firmly to the faith we profess," but what about those weaknesses which can lead to doubt and disobedience toward God, lovelessness toward our fellow man and preoccupation with ourselves? The high priest knows about such things, too. That's part of what makes him so great. In Jesus' life on earth when he took on our human nature and became true man, he also "was tempted in every way just as we are." From the beginning to the end of that earthly stay Jesus faced temptations more severe than we shall ever know. He felt the full pressure and pull as all the troops in hell's barracks with all the weapons from hell's arsenals stormed against him. He felt those temptations even more than we do because while we so often fall under temptation's first round, he remained standing to receive every assault.

Yet in all this he "was without sin." This thought can be taken two ways, both of which make good sense. It can mean that though tempted, he never yielded, but remained holy. Scripture rightly guards Christ's sinlessness zealously, reminding us in passages like 2 Corinthians 5:21 that he "had no sin" and 1 Peter 2:22 that "he committed no sin." A sinful Jesus could be no Savior and no great high priest.

Or the mention of his sinlessness can point to his perfect human nature. Unlike us, he had no "old Adam," no inherited sinful nature out of which temptations could arise. All the attacks came not from within, but from without, from Satan and the wicked world, so that Jesus could tell his disciples in John 14:30, "The prince of this world is coming. He has no hold on me." The point is that Jesus knows. Though repeated and very real temptation left his sinlessness unshaken, he knows what it's all about. From experience he knows what we face and his heart can well sympathize with us.

Give up such a high priest? Go back to Judaism where sinners dared not approach a holy God except through the mediation of a human high priest once a year? No, rather the author urges, "Let us then approach the throne of grace with confidence." It is God's throne we can approach, the seat of his infinite majesty and holy justice. Before this throne of splendor sinners shrink back in terror and stand mute in guilt. But with Christ our great high priest standing there, it becomes a "throne of grace" where believers "receive mercy and find grace to help us in our time of need."

In the nick of time, right when we need it, when our temptations come, we'll find what we need from him who knows just how to give it. We'll receive "mercy" there, God's love that looks at and offers help to believers overwhelmed by their own weaknesses. "Grace" will also be there, God's love, wholly undeserved, which pardons the guilty. To such a throne of grace we come boldly confessing sin and receiving forgiveness, pouring out sorrow and being comforted, laying down weaknesses and being strengthened, asking questions and being answered. But only because of the "great high priest" who has made full atonement for our sins.

5 **Every high priest is selected from among men and is appointed to represent them in matters related to God, to offer gifts and sacrifices for sins. [2]He is able to deal gently with those who are ignorant and are going astray, since he himself is subject to weakness. [3]This is why he has to offer sacrifices for his own sins, as well as for the sins of the people. [4]No one takes this honor upon himself; he must be called by God, just as Aaron was.**

The author advances the thought of Christ's superior priesthood by drawing a comparison between him and the high priests of Judaism. The Old Testament high priest was

The Costume of the High Priest

selected from among those whom he was to serve and his chief service was to "offer gifts and sacrifices for sins." He was to do this particularly on the Day of Atonement, as detailed in Leviticus 16.

In his dealings with sinners, he was to be gentle with those who were "ignorant" and "going astray." To "deal gently" means to balance one's feelings, avoiding both leniency and severity. Note that the author speaks of sinners "who are ignorant and are going astray," referring to Numbers 15:27-31, where distinction is made between sinning ignorantly and sinning defiantly.

Those who sinned defiantly and thus blasphemed God were to be cut off from Israel and carry their sins with them. Those who sinned ignorantly and unintentionally were to have their sins covered by the sacrifice brought on the Day of Atonement. The high priest, knowing from his own human experience the weaknesses with which his people had to grapple, could deal moderately with them.

But being human also had a disadvantage, since the high priest would have sins of his own. Leviticus 16 relates how the ritual on the Day of Atonement made provision for his sins. Before he sprinkled the blood of the goat on the mercy seat as an offering for the sins of his people, the high priest had to enter behind the veil into the Holy of Holies with the blood of a bullock "to make atonement for himself [and] his household" (Leviticus 16:17).

One other point the author makes about the Old Testament high priesthood: its divine appointment. In Exodus 28 and Leviticus 8 God established the Old Testament priesthood and called Aaron as its first high priest. Through Aaron's direct call God also marked his descendants as the ones from whom the high priests would come. No one took the office of the high priest upon himself. It was necessary to be called by God.

⁵So Christ also did not take upon himself the glory of becoming a high priest. But God said to him, "You are my Son; today I have become your Father." ⁶And he says in another place, "You are a priest forever, in the order of Melchizedek." ⁷During the days of Jesus' life on earth, he offered up prayers and petitions with loud cries and tears to the one who could save him from death, and he was heard because of his reverent submission. ⁸Although he was a son, he learned obedience from what he suffered and, once made perfect, he became the source of eternal salvation for all who obey him ¹⁰and was designated by God to be high priest in the order of Melchizedek.

The discerning reader can already see the direction the author is headed. How far superior to the Old Testament high priest Christ Jesus is! Was the question one about divine appointment to the priesthood? Let the reader listen to what God himself said in Psalm 2. There in verse seven the Father called Christ "my Son," something he never said of any Old Testament high priest. Also in Psalm 2, where God set forth the exalted position and authority of his Son as the Messiah, the author saw included a reference to that Son's priesthood.

For those concerned about authority and proper authorization the question should be settled. The Father, to whom the appointment belonged, had bestowed it upon his Son come into the flesh. Note that the greater word "glory" is used instead of "honor" in verse five because Christ's is the greater priesthood. Note, too, how Jesus in John 8:54 pointed out to the Jews how he obtained that glory, "If I glorify myself my glory means nothing. My Father, whom you claim as your God, is the one who glorifies me." Here was the greater high priest holding a glorious office as appointed by God himself.

With his quote from Psalm 110 the author reinforces the fact of Christ's divine appointment to the priesthood. In verse four of that Psalm of David God addresses the Messiah saying, "You are a priest forever in the order of Melchizedek." Aaron and his successors had their day in office and then passed away. This great high priest would hold his appointment "forever."

"In the order of Melchizedek," God said also of his Son's priesthood. Melchizedek is one of those mysteries of Holy Scripture, appearing only three times. In Genesis 14:18-20 he appears briefly as he meets and blesses Abraham returning from rescuing Lot. There he is called both "King of Salem" and "priest of God Most High." In Psalm 110:4 David refers to him even more briefly and by inspiration sees in him a type of Christ, who would be both King and Priest. And in the letter to the Hebrews the reference again appears, in much greater detail, as we shall see later.

Did those Hebrew Christians want to revert to Judaism with its high priesthood? Here is a high priest far greater, one who is appointed forever. Here is one whose priesthood goes back far before Aaron's and combines both a king's power and a priest's sacrifice, just as with Melchizedek in the days of Abraham.

Was there a question about sympathizing with his people? Let the reader think back to "the days of Jesus' life on earth." Didn't the great high priest Jesus know something about the human frailties of those he represented? Had he not taken on their human nature? The author points us particularly to one instance, our Lord's great crisis in Gethsemane on the night before his crucifixion.

The author piles up the words, giving us under the Spirit's guidance even more details than recorded in the four Gospels. "Prayers," expressions of needs, became "petitions," urgent requests, a word used of suppliants carrying an olive branch as a symbol of extreme need. From Christ's lips also came "loud cries," literally cries he did not want to utter, but which were wrung out of him by extreme agony. From his eyes came "tears" as visible signs of his woe. The anguish and the agony deepen till they lead to his sweat "like drops of blood falling to the ground" (Luke 22:44). Did any of those Hebrew Christians think they were alone? Was persecution's pressure rubbing their souls sore? Here was one who, utterly alone, had gone through more than they would ever know. Here was one who would know just how to help them.

To whom and for what did the great high priest pray in the Garden of Gethsemane? Both are answered in the words, "to him who could save him from death." As the darkness of a world's sin wrapped around him and the horror of a world's damnation washed over him, his human nature shrank from the task. This was not refusal, but recoil. In perfect obedience he adds to his fervent praying the words recorded in Matthew 26:42, "My father, if it is not possible for this cup to be taken away unless I drink it, may your will be done." And his prayer was heard "because of his reverent submission." Because he was completely attuned and perfectly submissive to his Father's holy will, Jesus' prayer was heard and answered. The Father's answer was not to relieve his Son of the cross, but to ready him for it, even sending an angel from heaven to strengthen him (Luke 22:43).

Just think of the powerful miracle and profound mystery involved in all of this. He who is God's Son from all eternity takes on human form and suffers. He who as God's Son perfectly obeys the Father from all eternity now learns "obedience from what he suffered." Jesus did not first learn to obey here. That he always knew as already he showed when as a twelve-year-old in the temple he stated to his earthly parents, "Didn't you know I had to be in my Father's house?"

Now he learned the full cost of that obedience, carrying it to a point beyond which it could not be taken. "He became obedient to death — even death on a cross!" Philippians 2:8 succinctly summarizes. Submissively praying, miraculously strengthened, he goes in obedience to the cross, the tomb, the throne.

"Once made perfect," (or more literally: "having reached his goal" of cross, tomb and throne) this great high priest "became the source of eternal salvation for all who obey him." Aaron and his successors were sinful, making atonement for their own sins first, but this one is sinless in character and perfect in obedience. Aaron and his successors offered sacrifices year after year to atone for sins, but this one offered only once and it was enough. Aaron and his successors brought animal blood whose only power lay in its pointing ahead to this great priest whose "blood purifies us from every sin" (1 John 1:7). Here is the priest who by his suffering and death was "made perfect," that is, has reached the assigned goal of being the "source of eternal salvation."

"For all who obey him" matches the thought of Christ's obedience and offers no difficulty when we let 1 John 3:22,23 explain, "We obey his commands and do what pleases him. And this is his command: to believe in the name of his Son, Jesus Christ." Faith is obedience to God and is worked in the individual by God's grace through word and sacrament. It is God's gift that man can live with God and for God through faith's obedience.

Were the Hebrew Christians thinking about deserting such a superior high priest, the one designated by God himself for this high office as prophesied already in Psalm 110:4 and completed by his sacrifice on the cross? Be warned — to go back to Judaism with its high priesthood would be to go back to something far inferior and finally fatal.

And what about us who read these words of the inspired author today? Though priests and altars, persecution and sore pressure may not be our particular problems today, still temptation is ever before us. May God, who alone can work faith, give us that trust and confidence which always cries out, "To whom save thee, who canst alone for sin atone, Lord, shall I flee?"

WARNING:
DO NOT BE IMMATURE OR BECOME LAZY

[11]**We have much to say about this, but it is hard to explain because you are slow to learn.** [12]**In fact, though by this time you ought to be teachers, you need someone to teach you the elementary truths of God's word all over again. You need milk, not solid food!** [13]**Anyone who lives on milk, being still an infant, is not acquainted with the teaching about righteousness.** [14]**But solid food is for the mature, who by constant use have trained themselves to distinguish good from evil.**

Again the author's pastoral heart shines through. He had so much to say to them about Christ being a high priest like Melchizedek. But it would be difficult. The problem lay not with the subject matter that was unclear or a presentation that was unskilled, but with the hearers. "You are slow to learn," the author scolded, using a word that meant numbed or dulled. Ears that once had been eager to hear were now dulled and unable to receive deep truths. Like a pastor with a less than perfect flock, the author lovingly scolds his readers. His intention is not to gripe at them because of their sluggish hearing, but to get those ears ready to hear that glorious subject of Christ's higher priesthood.

Did the readers realize how tough they were making it for the author? By this time in their Christianity they should have become teachers. To be able to teach implies being well grounded in and having a firm grasp of the subject matter. But look at those Hebrew Christians. Instead of being teachers, they needed someone to teach them "the elementary truths of God's word all over again." Instead of advancing beyond the ABCs to more and deeper truths, they had gone backward, requiring someone to review the basics with them again. They were back at the baby stage where spiritual stomachs could handle only milk. How could the author feed such babies the "solid food" of Christ's higher priesthood?

Everyone knows that, just as an infant can drink only milk, so believers who suffer from retarded maturity can handle only the simplest spiritual truths. Such believers are "not acquainted with the teaching about righteousness," knowing little about Christian truth and as a result having a hard time distinguishing between right and wrong. Recall Paul's words in Ephesians 4:14 about "infants, tossed back and forth by the waves, and blown here and there by every wind of teaching and by the cunning and craftiness of men in their deceitful scheming."

Do you see the author's pastoral heart? He is not belittling babies in the faith or disparaging fundamental truths. There will always be babies and adults in the faith, and God's word contains both milk for the babies and solid food for the adults. But babies are not to remain babies nor is adulthood to revert back to childhood. Growth is necessary, such as can come only from "constant use" and training. A spiritual exercise program was essential with the only piece of equipment required being the word. That is what the author wishes for his readers so that he can lead them into deeper truths.

Don't his words ring in our ears, too? There is no such thing as standing still in Christianity. Whether a believer marches forward or merely marks time depends much on his connection with God's word. God's deep truths are not revealed to the casual, careless reader, but to the careful, constant one. Regardless how hectic our life is or how fast each day flies by, we need to find regular opportunity for serious Bible study. Those who do will find milk giving way to meat and childhood to adulthood.

6 **Therefore let us leave the elementary teachings about Christ and go on to maturity, not laying again the foundation of repentance from acts that lead to death, and of faith in God, [2]instruction about baptisms, the laying on of hands, the resurrection of the dead, and eternal judgment. [3]And God permitting, we will do so.**

The author, with his rebuke delivered and hopefully effective, is ready to move on. His desire is not to abandon the ABCs about Christ, but to build on them. What value is there in laying and then relaying a foundation without ever erecting anything on it? So it's "let us go on to maturity," to a stage beyond childhood and to matters that are more mature. The Greek form for "let us go on" has the thought of the believer not doing this advancing on his own, but being carried along to maturity. This is the work of the Spirit through the instructing and powering word.

Certainly the foundation was important. A brief look at the items which the author lists among the "elementary teachings about Christ" shows how important. There is "repentance from acts that lead to death." "Repentance" signifies an inner change of the heart, a turning away from sin to contrition, from guilt to pardon. "Acts that lead to death" vividly reminded the readers of their former state, of how as unbelievers they had been "dead in transgressions and sins" (Ephesians 2:1) and deserving the "wages of sin" which is "death" (Romans 6:23).

Coupled with this repentance is "faith in God." The two belong together. There can be no genuine turning away from sin unless the sinner is first turned to a faith based on God and his promises. Repentance always looks in two directions, backward in sincere contrition over sin and forward in firm trust in God's pardon.

Next the author mentions "instruction" or doctrinal teaching. Those readers had received "instruction about baptisms." The plural might refer to the instructions given and distinctions made between the various ceremonial washings prevalent among the Jews and the true baptism commanded by Jesus. Or since baptism is a highly individual matter, the plural may refer to the baptism of each individual. Connected with baptism to this day is "the laying on of hands." The book of Acts particularly shows how in a number of different situations the laying on of hands was a symbol of blessing being given (Acts 8:17, 9:12, 13:3, 19:6).

There was also instruction about "the resurrection of the dead, and eternal judgment." From the beginning Christianity was a religion centered around resurrection and judgment. He who has been brought in faith to the filled cross and emptied tomb of Christ would know and cherish the sure hope of resurrection from the dead and of a favorable verdict in heaven's court. Though he must still face death and judgment, it's with victory assured.

All these areas from repentance to eternal judgment are great themes and teachings essential to Christian life. What the author points out, though, is that they are only the ABCs in the alphabet of faith. It was time to go on and that's what the author intended to do, "God permitting." The author does more than use pious phraseology for a polite nod in

God's direction. He clearly sees that only God can sensitize the dulled ears of his hearers and lend success to the presentation of the additional instruction he has in mind.

[4]It is impossible for those who have once been enlightened, who have tasted the heavenly gift, who have shared in the Holy Spirit, [5]who have tasted the goodness of the word of God and the powers of the coming age, [6]if they fall away, to be brought back to repentance, because to their loss they are crucifying the Son of God all over again and subjecting him to public disgrace. [7]Land that drinks in the rain often falling on it and that produces a crop useful to those for whom it is farmed receives the blessing of God. [8]But land that produces thorns and thistles is worthless and is in danger of being cursed. In the end it will be burned.

This section along with 10:26-31, presents part of the teaching of what is called "the sin against the Holy Ghost." Here is a section that has been much discussed and often debated, but the best is to let the words speak for themselves.

The author is writing about people who had once believed, people who had actually tasted the gospel's sweetness and experienced its blessedness. They had been "enlightened," having the darkness of their hearts replaced with the shining truths of him whom John 8:12 calls "the light of the world."

They had also "tasted the heavenly gift." In John 4:10, speaking to the woman at the well in Samaria, Jesus called himself "the gift of God." God so loved that he gave his Son from heaven, and these people had tasted the joy of that heavenly gift.

Furthermore, they had "shared in the Holy Spirit." By the Spirit's sanctifying work through the gospel they had faith to see and taste the sweet gift of the Savior. So the author reminded them when he said they had "tasted the goodness of the word of God." There is no other word as "good." Only through God's utterance does the Spirit come to and dwell in human hearts.

And finally they had tasted the "powers of the coming age." The word with its power had worked effects in their hearts which would endure into eternity. Paul said it well in 1 Corinthians 2:9: "No eye has seen, no ear has heard, no mind has conceived what God has prepared for those who love him, but God has revealed it to us by his Spirit."

So it is believers of whom the author sadly speaks, but of believers who "fall away." This word, used only here in the New Testament, means to fall to the side, to fall completely away. Here's no panicky Peter pouring out denials in weakness. This is a deliberate conscious repudiation of what is known to be true. Here are believers stepping deliberately back into unbelief's darkness and willfully discarding the heavenly gift of Christ.

Of such the author states, "It is impossible for those . . . to be brought back to repentance." Such turncoat believers rip Christ from their hearts and raise him up on the cross for all to scoff at. To their loss, they join the ranks of those who crucified the Son of God.

With "Son of God" the author points out the enormity of their crime. Like the Sanhedrin, against better knowledge, they nail the God-man to the tree and parade in scorn beneath his form. How much worse is the disgrace when it comes from those who once were friends. The word of an insider carries tremendous impact, and when that insider becomes a detractor, how much more cutting those words can be. For such there is no repentance.

Notice the author did not say there was no salvation for them. Christ's sacrifice paid for the sins against the Holy Ghost, too, but with their deliberate turning away from what they knew by experience to be true, they had made further working of repentance impossible and deprived themselves of the salvation that Christ purchased for them too. For those who have tried everything Christ has to offer and then turn away, the Holy Spirit can do nothing more. Our limited minds have a hard time conceiving of something being impossible for an omnipotent God and of someone deliberately abandoning what he knows to be true. But it can happen, the author states, and it could happen to those Hebrew Christians. By skillfully switching from "you" and "us" to "they" in this section, the author shows that his readers have not yet fallen into this sin. But he's concerned that they might and earnestly warns them against willfully abandoning Christ and his treasures for the safety of Judaism.

Would an illustration help the readers understand the divine judgment involved? Then let them picture a plot of ground drinking in the frequent rain and producing crops as expected by the owners. Such a plot receives the continuing care of the farmer so that it may yield for years to come.

With "blessing of God" the author reveals that he has more than a field in mind. He's moving from the lesser to the greater, from fields to the hearts of men. Fruitful fields are a picture of the believer whose life bears the visible fruit produced by the invisible heart of faith.

But let those hearts receive the same care. Let them be rained on and carefully cultivated and yet produce no more than thorns and thistles — and the judgment eventually comes. Such hearts have been tested and found worthless. They are headed, not for cultivation but for cursing. Their end is not harvest, but fiery destruction. The illustration speaks of judgment, and the application to those who "fall away" is obvious.

The footnote in the NIV Bible (Or *repentance while*) indicates another possible translation of this difficult passage. Beginning at verse 4, the passage would then read: "It is impossible for those who have once been enlightened, who have tasted . . . shared . . . tasted . . . if they fall away, to be brought back to repentance, WHILE to their loss they are crucifying the Son of God all over again and subjecting him to public disgrace."

In other words, repentance is impossible for such people as long as they continue in their deliberate rejecting of the crucified Christ as their Savior. They cut themselves off from the grace of God in Christ Jesus, although they had been recipients of that grace and formerly were believers. This would leave room for the possibility of repentance once they desist from their senseless rebellion against their Lord and Savior. There is no conflict between this interpretation and the warning that will follow in 10:26-31.

It is significant to note that either interpretation of this passage clearly rejects the opinion that a true believer can never fall from the faith and be lost ("Once a believer, always a believer"). Here we have a clear warning that believers can fall and be lost. "So, if you think you are standing firm, be careful that you don't fall!" (1 Corinthians 10:12)

Every pastor has encountered those who fear they have committed this "unforgivable sin against the Holy Ghost." They worry that there is no hope for them, that there is no more chance for repentance and that hell's fires are their destination. God's love in Christ Jesus is still the answer for them, God's love which paid for sin. Also of practical comfort is the observation that those who fear they have sinned against the Holy Ghost have not. Their very fear is proof they have not. Those who have don't worry about it. It's only in hell that their fear will begin, never again to end.

⁹Even though we speak like this, dear friends, we are confident of better things in your case — things that accompany salvation.

[10]God is not unjust; he will not forget your work and the love you have shown him as you have helped his people and continue to help them. [11]We want each of you to show this same diligence to the very end, in order to make your hope sure. [12]We do not want you to become lazy, but to imitate those who through faith and patience inherit what has been promised.

The warning had been stern, but the situation was not hopeless. "Dear friends" or "beloved" the author could still call them, exhibiting the love that lay behind his warning and also expressing the confidence that the readers had not fallen away to the dire extent just mentioned. Yes, things had declined and were not as they should have been, but the author could still think positively about these Hebrew Christians. "We are confident of better things," he could say, "things that accompany salvation." It wasn't destruction, but salvation; not curse, but blessing; not a barren field covered with thorns and thistles, but one fruitful and productive which the author confidently saw when he looked at his readers.

Such confidence could rest on only one ground, the abiding character of God. "God is not unjust," the author states. He whose righteous judgment does not ignore spiritual rebellion cannot overlook a heart of faith and a life of love either. "Work" and "love" belong ever together. When God looks at deeds, he sees beneath the surface. He looks into the heart, noting the motive behind the work. Only love springing from faith can make a believer's work acceptable to God.

Notice how the author agrees with the thought expressed in 1 John 4:19-21, "We love because he first loved us. If anyone says, 'I love God,' yet hates his brother, he is a liar. For anyone who does not love his brother, whom he has seen, cannot love God, whom he has not seen. And he has given us this command: Whoever loves God must also love his brother." The readers were actually showing love to God when they helped his people and continued to help them. Later in 10:32-34 the author explains those deeds of love. He writes, "Remember those earlier days after you had received the light, when you stood your ground in a great contest in the face of suffering. Sometimes you were publicly exposed to insult and persecution; at other times you stood side by side with those who were so treated. You sympathized with those in prison and joyfully accepted the confiscation of your property, because you knew that you yourselves had better and lasting possessions." The author saw their faith in deeds done solely out of love for the sake of God's glory. He was confident the righteous Lord could see it, too.

Besides confidence, the author had concern. There was something he wanted, something his pastoral heart strongly desired for each one of them. Just as God yearns for and watches over individuals, so did the author. The diligence they had shown in loving deeds for each other was to be matched by an equal diligence for strengthening one another's faith. Those believers had a ways to go and the way would not be easy. Good beginnings are not what count, but the right endings.

So the writer urges diligence "to the very end," diligence "to make your hope sure." The hope of eternal glory, won and promised by the Savior, can never burn too brightly in a believer's heart. Fuller assurance comes through fuller use of the word in which that hope is revealed and on which it rests. Let that strengthening word be our diligent concern till Christ returns and hope becomes glorious reality for each one of us.

Lazy ears lead eventually to lazy faith and hope. The author had noted a decline in faith and hope setting in among his readers, so he urged immediate steps to counteract it. One remedy is to "imitate those who through faith and patience inherit what has been promised." Strength can be found in looking at the examples of fellow believers who are around us or who have gone before us. Later in chapter 11 the author will unveil the examples of some of those Old Testament heroes of faith. "Imitate them," he says. "They inherit," he says, that is, they have firm possession of "what has been promised." Those precious promises, given so often and in so many ways, were theirs "through faith and patience."

One cannot speak about God's promises without speaking about faith. Man needs faith to embrace God's promises and God's promises work and continue to work that faith till it becomes sight in heaven. Faith and patience also go together. Patience is the quality of putting up with what people do, of being undismayed in difficulty. Connect patience with faith and you have a steadiness that makes it through in spite of all dangers. Such faith and hope the author earnestly desired for his readers as he pointed them to the examples of those who had fought and won. We who travel heaven's highway centuries later can also gain encouragement from the reminder that "we are treading where the saints have trod."

13When God made his promise to Abraham, since there was no one greater for him to swear by, he swore by himself, 14saying, "I will surely bless you and give you many descendants." 15And so after waiting patiently, Abraham received what was promised. 16Men swear by someone greater than themselves, and the oath confirms what is said and puts an end to all argument. 17Because God wanted to make the unchanging nature of his purpose very clear to the heirs of what was promised, he confirmed it with an oath. 18God did this so that, by two unchangeable things in which it is impossible for God to lie, we who have fled to take hold of the

hope offered to us may be greatly encouraged. [19]We have this hope as an anchor for the soul, firm and secure. It enters the inner sanctuary behind the curtain, [20]where Jesus, who went before us, has entered in our behalf. He has become a high priest forever, in the order of Melchizedek.

Could there be a more effective example of inheriting God's promise through faith and patience than Abraham? To the Hebrew readers the example was doubly effective since they were the descendants of Abraham. For us, too, as believers in Christ, the promised Seed of Abraham, the example has deep meaning. What promises Abraham had received from God — the promise of a great nation to come from his loins, and best of all, the Savior to come from his descendants. But long years passed, 25 in all, and nothing happened. It would have been easy to give up, but Abraham pressed on with an unwavering trust in a God who could not change and a promise that could not fail. And then it happened! Isaac was born!

Years later when God came seeking not Isaac's sacrifice, but Abraham's heart, that faith still did not waver. At that time God repeated his gracious promise to Abraham and even sealed it with an oath as Genesis 22:15-18 records. What love and concern God shows for his own. To further assure Abraham, he condescends to human custom and uses an oath. Behind his promise which was already reliable because it had come from an infallible God, he now places his very own integrity. Oaths work because they call upon someone greater to witness the truth and punish the lie. Since God had no one greater to swear by, he confirmed his promise to Abraham with an oath based on himself. God wants his promises to be trusted and gives his children every incentive to do so.

Abraham endured and received the promise. In the birth of his son Isaac and of his grandchildren Jacob and Esau he saw the beginning of the great nation. In Isaac's birth he saw also the coming fulfillment of the Savior's birth. In all those who share his trust in this Savior, Abraham has his seed multiplied beyond measure.

And when Abraham died, he saw the promise in full. In Matthew 8:11 Jesus, the promised Seed of Abraham, told the Jews, "I say to you that many will come from the east and the west, and will take their places at the feast with Abraham, Isaac and Jacob in the kingdom of heaven." In that heavenly kingdom all true heirs of salvation will join Abraham before the throne of him whom Revelation 13:8 describes as "the Lamb that was slain from the creation of the world."

All believers are in the same position as Abraham. They have the glorious promise of salvation from God, and they are to hold fast to that promise. They have God's oath standing behind the promise. The readers knew the value of human oaths. A sworn statement, appealing to God as witness, settles things for man. Contradictions have to cease and questions stop when an oath is taken.

If this is true with man, how much more so with God. To give men more assurance God descended to their level. In his grace he put behind his already unshakable promise of salvation his uncompromising oath. Could he have made his plan of salvation any clearer? What witness might he give in addition to the promise itself and the divine oath behind it? These two, the promise and the oath, are "unchangeable things in which it is impossible for God to lie."

Unlike human beings who often have trouble with the truth, "God . . . does not lie" (Titus 1:2). When he offers two witnesses, as men usually require to make things legal, you can trust him. Those two witnesses are his promise of salvation given to Abraham and to us and his oath behind it. Both are without falsehood because God simply cannot lie. Both offer the strongest encouragement possible to those "who have fled to take hold of the hope offered to us." Like mariners fleeing the tempest, guilty sinners run from judgment's storm into the safe harbor of Jesus Christ. "The hope offered to us" refers to Jesus Christ himself as the next picture plainly shows.

Few things were more important to the sailor in a storm than a good anchor and a good ground for it. Believers in Christ have both. They have "an anchor for the soul, firm and secure." Like some anchor whose strong flukes cannot be twisted out of shape, so we have in Christ an absolutely strong and reliable hope. Also like some anchor which holds only when fixed in the right ground, so we have our hope anchored in the right spot. He's in "the inner sanctuary behind the curtain," a reference to the Holy of Holies, into which only the high priest entered and only on the Day of Atonement.

Our High Priest is now on the other side of the curtain in heaven. There he "who went before us" waits for us. And as he waits, he pleads for us. With his perfect payment for sins on our behalf he has split the curtain separating God and man and made it possible for us also to enter that heavenly sanctuary. The high priests from Aaron's line could not compete with Jesus, the eternal high priest in the order of Melchizedek.

To this day and to the final day men will hope. That's their nature. But hope to be worthwhile needs a ground that is real. Those who by the Spirit's working have anchored their hope on Christ can join in Paul's confident words of 2 Timothy 1:12: "I know whom I have believed, and am convinced that he is able to guard what I have entrusted to him for that day." Meanwhile, as we wait for that day and are battered by the storms, God help us ever to pray,

65

> His oath, his covenant and blood
> Support me in the whelming flood.
> In every high and stormy gale
> My anchor holds within the veil.
> On Christ, the solid Rock, I stand;
> All other ground is sinking sand.

He Is a Priest Superior in Office

7 **This Melchizedek was king of Salem and priest of God Most High. He met Abraham returning from the defeat of the kings and blessed him, [2]and Abraham gave him a tenth of everything. First, his name means "king of righteousness"; then also, "king of Salem" means "king of peace." [3]Without father or mother, without genealogy, without beginning of days or end of life, like the Son of God he remains a priest forever.**

Why all this stress on Christ's high priesthood? The author has already briefly alluded to it in 4:14 and three times (in 5:6,10; 6:20) described it as a priesthood after the order of Melchizedek. Now in our chapter he dwells on it in great detail. For us it may be difficult to realize how central the priesthood was to the Jewish religion and how tightly the Jews clung to it. The appeal to leave Christianity with its imminent persecution for Judaism with its eminent priesthood must have been strong. To counteract this pull the author convincingly presents the superiority of Christ's priesthood by pointing to his office and showing that he was a priest not after the order of Levi, but of Melchizedek.

Melchizedek is one of those shadowy persons in Scripture about whom we would like to know more. Almost 2,000 years before Christ's birth we find him first mentioned in a seemingly inconsequential scene with Abraham. Then there is nothing more until almost 1,000 years later when David

The Offerings of Melchizedek

picks up the name in Psalm 110:4. Now it's almost A.D. 70 when his name surfaces again in Hebrews.

Four short verses over 2,000 years, and yet look what conclusions the author of the letter to the Hebrews draws from them. Under the inspiration of the Spirit the author again amazes us by revealing how Christ-centered the whole Old Testament is. In both Genesis 14 and Psalm 110 with their references to Melchizedek the author sees unmistakable reference to Jesus Christ and his superior high priesthood. Were those Jewish Christians thinking of reverting to Judaism with its vaunted and revered Levitical priesthood? Then let them stop to reflect on those four verses in their own Old Testament and what they said about the superiority of this high priest in the order of Melchizedek.

Both Genesis 14 and Psalm 110 tell us little about Melchizedek's person. Nor is this important. These verses do tell us about his being a type of the coming Christ. In Genesis 14 Melchizedek meets Abraham, who is returning from rescuing Lot and the inhabitants of Sodom and Gomorrah from the warring kings of the East. There this shadowy figure is described as "king of Salem" and "priest of God Most High." "Salem" could be the city of Jerusalem as in Psalm 76:2 or it could be some other city. "Priest of God Most High" tells us that he knew and served the true, almighty God. Like Abraham, Melchizedek was one of those people in idolatrous Canaan who still held the true faith handed on by Noah. For us the significance lies in Melchizedek's being both king and priest, something which no priest from Levi's line ever was.

His actions were also significant and revealed his priesthood. Melchizedek blessed Abraham and received from him a tenth of the spoils taken from the defeated kings. Here was something for those Hebrew Christians to think about!

Their great father Abraham obviously recognized and honored the priesthood of Melchizedek. For everyone knows that the greater blesses the lesser and that the lesser pays tithes to the greater. Significant, too, were his names. "Melchizedek" means "king of righteousness," while "king of Salem" means "king of peace." Here was not just a king, but one whose kingship was totally in harmony with his priesthood.

Doesn't this make us think of our heavenly King and Priest? Christ's name, as Jeremiah 23:6 reminds us, is "the Lord our Righteousness." He came to prepare what sinful man was lacking, offering himself as our Priest to make us righteous before God. As a result he truly is the "Prince of peace" whom Isaiah foretold in 9:6. At his birth the angels could proclaim "on earth peace to men" (Luke 2:14), and in John 14:27 this wonderful King himself could tell his disciples of all times, "Peace I leave with you; my peace I give unto you. I do not give to you as the world gives." Priest and King he is in a most wonderful way; cross and throne are interwoven.

What Scripture does *not* say about Melchizedek is also significant. There is no record of his father or mother, no genealogical table, nothing about his birth or death. All these were items of utmost importance to high priests and in fact to any priests in Levi's line. To be a priest one had to prove his descent, not only from Levi, but from Aaron's priestly family within the tribe of Levi. In Ezra 2:61-63 we are told that the descendants of Hobaiah, Hakkoz and Barzillai were excluded from the priesthood because they could not locate their family records.

But about Melchizedek's genealogy Scripture says nothing. It shows him appearing and vanishing and tells us that "like the Son of God he remains a priest forever." That's the point! Melchizedek is like the Son of God, the divine Christ, of whom he serves as a type. Scripture has recorded and omitted what it did about Melchizedek to show us something about Christ the superior high priest. He's a high priest who has no beginning or end, one whose office depends not on his family descent, and whose service never ends. He truly "remains a priest forever."

4Just think how great he was: Even the patriarch Abraham gave him a tenth of the plunder! 5Now the law requires the descendants of Levi who become priests to collect a tenth from the people — that is, their brothers — even though their brothers are descended from Abraham. 6This man, however, did not trace his descent from Levi, yet he collected a tenth from Abraham and blessed him who had the promises. 7And without doubt the lesser person is blessed by the greater. 8In the one case, the tenth is collected by men who die; but in the other case, by him who is declared to be living. 9 One might even say that Levi, who collects the tenth, paid the tenth through Abraham, 10because when Melchizedek met Abraham, Levi was still in the body of his ancestor.

The scriptural facts about Melchizedek have been introduced. Now the author elaborates to show how far superior Melchizedek's priesthood was to that of the Levitical priesthood. Could anyone dispute that the patriarch Abraham was great? Yet consider how in Melchizedek he met someone obviously greater, for he gave this priest "a tenth of the plunder." Under inspiration the author gives more details than Moses did. In Genesis 14:20 Moses stated, "Abram gave him a tenth of everything," while the author of Hebrews describes it as "a tenth of the plunder," the top portion from the heaped up spoils of victory.

There was no mistaking this gesture. Jewish Christians knew about the tithe and to whom it was paid. The Mosaic Law in Numbers 18:21,24 gave the Levitical priesthood the authority to collect the tithe from their fellow Israelites. Though they were all brothers as descendants of Abraham, yet by law the Levitical priesthood had authority and superiority in the matter of the tithe.

Now consider Melchizedek. Long before Levi was born and the priesthood began, long before the Mosaic Law was in force and the tithe demanded, Abraham gave it voluntarily to Melchizedek. Not from brothers, but from great father Abraham did this tithe come, unsolicited and undemanded. Besides accepting the tithe from Abraham, Melchizedek showed his superiority by blessing him as recorded in Genesis 14. Again when Abraham received blessings from this divine envoy, there was no mistaking who was greater. The general principle is that only the greater can bless the lesser.

Besides receiving the tithe from and giving a blessing to Abraham, Melchizedek showed his greatness in another way. Only for a brief while could the Levitical priests serve, clothed with the dignity of their office and collecting the tithe. From the present tense "is collected" which the author used, we sense that perhaps the Old Testament priesthood was still functioning in Jerusalem. If so, then this letter had to be written before A.D. 70 when the Roman army destroyed Jerusalem, dispersed the Jewish people, disbanded the priesthood. At any rate, while the Levitical high priesthood functioned, it was a succession of dying men, but Melchizedek's priesthood had no end. Though he, too, was mortal, Scripture nowhere records the fact of his death and in this way uses him as a type of Christ. Melchizedek's superior priesthood found its fulfillment in Christ, the High Priest who had neither predecessor nor successor.

Did the Hebrew readers follow the argument? If Melchizedek was greater than Abraham, then he must also be greater than the priests who were descendants of Abraham through his great-grandson Levi. Of course, Levi did not in person pay the tithe to Melchizedek. For when Abraham met Melchizedek, Isaac had not yet been conceived and Levi therefore was still in great-grandfather Abraham's loins. Nor did Levi ever collect tithes in person from the Israelites. The tithe came years later when his descendant Aaron was made the first high priest and the Mosaic Law was given. But just as Levi collected the tithe through his descendants, so he paid them through his forefather.

Did anyone want to claim that the Levitical priesthood was superior and that to return to it was the better course of action? Then let him recall how in Abraham Levi had bowed to a superior high priest named Melchizedek. Above all, let him look to Jesus, the High Priest forever in the order of Melchizedek. He is the supreme blesser. It was he who gave the blessing of Numbers 6:22-27 to the priests of Levi and through them to the people. It was he who in Luke 24:50 "lifted up his hands and blessed them" at the ascension. It is he whose high priestly hands stretch out in endless blessing over his own. And it is to him that all true believers like their spiritual forefather Abraham will give due honor and homage.

11If perfection could have been attained through the Levitical priesthood (for on the basis of it the law was given to the people), why was there still need for another priest to come — one in the order of Melchizedek, not in the order of Aaron? 12For when there is a change of the priesthood, there must also be a change of the law. 13He of whom these things are said belonged to a different tribe, and no one from that tribe has ever served at the altar. 14For it is clear that our Lord descended from Judah, and in regard to that tribe Moses said nothing about priests. 15And what we have said is even more clear if another priest like Melchizedek appears, 16one who has become a priest not on the basis of a regulation as to his ancestry but on the basis of the power of an indestructible life.

¹⁷For it is declared: "You are a priest forever, in the order of Melchizedek."

Step by step the author has been leading up to the superiority of Christ's high priesthood. If Melchizedek was superior, surely the high priest to whom he pointed must be also. To show this fact, the author points to the purpose of the priesthood. Its function was to make sinful man acceptable before God, something the Levitical priesthood could not do. Though God gave the Mosaic Law in support of this priesthood, laying down regulation after regulation about its operation, yet the fact remained that the Levitical priesthood was incomplete. It could not make man acceptable before God. All it could do with the blood of its repeated animal sacrifices was to point ahead to the one great sacrifice by which sinners would be cleansed.

Because of this inability the Levitical priesthood had to be replaced. And it was. David had spoken about the replacing in Psalm 110, which was written long after the Levitical priesthood had been in force. There was to be a new high priest, not like Aaron, but like Melchizedek. Boldly the author goes on. If the priesthood has been superseded, what about the Mosaic Law given in support of it? That, too, was changed. No more does the Mosaic covenant stand, as chapter eight will show. Would those Jewish Christians want to go back to an incomplete priesthood and an outdated covenant when before them stood the superior high priest who perfectly fulfilled the priesthood and reunites God and man forever?

The ancestry of this high priest showed also that the Law had been changed. Nowhere did the Law make provision for anyone outside the tribe of Levi to be a priest, much less offer sacrifices at the great altar outside the temple. Yet everyone knew that this high priest "descended from Ju-

dah. " Both the genealogical tables given in Matthew 1 and
Luke 3 and the account of his birth in Luke 2 record that
Jesus was from Judah. Our Lord "descended from Judah,"
the author says, using a word that means to rise like a star or
spring up like a shoot out of a root, and that reminds us of
God's promise in Jeremiah 23:5, "I will raise up to David a
righteous Branch." "Our" Lord the author also writes, gent-
ly drawing the readers to their confession of this great priest.
The Law has been changed; no longer are the Levites priests.
One from Judah now serves and in a far superior way.

All that has been said about the incompleteness of the
Levitical priesthood, the repealing of the Law of Moses and
the descent of Christ from Judah clearly marks Jesus as a
superior high priest. Something else makes this even clearer.
Christ "has become a priest not on the basis of a regulation
as to his ancestry but on the basis of an indestructible life."
Because the Levitical priesthood was mortal, laws about
succession were needed. Laws made the descendants of Levi
priests and laws kept this priesthood going when replace-
ments were needed.

With this greater high priest it is far different. No law made
him priest and no laws are needed about successors. His life is
"indestructible." He is the God-man, life itself. He can say, "I
am the life," as he did in John 14:6, and really mean it. His is
an eternal priesthood which can actually give life without
end, and his priestly heart links him to us with a love that
death can never sever. God himself said so already through
King David. In Psalm 110:4 he marked his eternal Son as the
superior replacement for Levi's mortal line when he testified,
"You are a priest forever, in the order of Melchizedek."

**18The former regulation is set aside because it was weak and
useless 19(for the law made nothing perfect), and a better hope is
introduced, by which we draw near to God.**

The author focuses more sharply on this high priest and his great priesthood in order to show their superiority. First he points to the better result of Christ's high priestly work. In verse 12 he spoke about this great high priest's coming as necessitating a change in the laws and regulations governing the Levitical priesthood. Now he makes it even more emphatic. He says, "The former regulation is set aside." "To set aside" means more than to try to patch and repair so that it fits something new. It's a legal term which involves complete cancellation. The Mosaic Law supporting the Levitical priesthood was no longer in effect, but set completely aside.

For good reason, the author says, because "it was weak and useless." Even though God had given the Mosaic Law, it was characterized by a certain weakness and uselessness. Its chief weakness was that it could make nothing perfect. Note that the author does not say that the Law served no useful purpose. Both the Law and the priesthood it supported preceded and paved the way for something better. They cast shadows ahead to and pointed out details about the better high priest coming. But that was the extent of their purpose. They could not make men right with God through animal sacrifices or change men's hearts to make them want to walk the way of God's commandments. Such results could come only from the work of the high priest in the order of Melchizedek.

"A better hope is introduced, by which we draw near to God," the author states, pointing to the results of this high priest's work. God annulled the former priesthood and introduced the better hope. Later the author will more fully explain this better hope on which we can rest our confidence for eternal life. Here it is enough to point out that it is based on the all-atoning sacrifice of the great high priest. When he shed his blood on Calvary's cross, the sins which like some thick curtain separated man from God were removed. His blood like some invisible scissors rent that curtain in two, so sinners can draw confidently near their God both in this world and in the coming one. What further need is there for an Old Testament priesthood and animal sacrifices when the high priest to which they pointed has come and done perfectly what they could not do.

[20] And it was not without an oath! Others became priests without any oath, [21] but he became a priest with an oath when God said to him: "The Lord has sworn and will not change his mind: 'You are a priest forever.' " [22] Because of this oath, Jesus has become the guarantee of a better covenant.

Next the author points out the superiority of Christ's high priesthood by referring to the oath on which it was based. God gave laws governing and supporting the Levitical priesthood, but not once did he issue an oath guaranteeing its uninterrupted operation. In fact, the Levitical priesthood was temporary and was made to be replaced. But about his Son's high priesthood God had sworn already in the time of David. In Psalm 110:4 the wording of the oath is not revealed, but what that oath supported certainly is. "You are a priest forever," he swore. Not only was David's Son and Lord to be a "priest," but a priest "forever." His would be a permanent priesthood, never ending, never changing, and consequently far superior to the temporary Levitical priesthood. Not only had God said so, which should have been enough to guarantee the fact, but he had also sworn and would not change his mind.

Just think of what this oath about Christ's permanent priesthood assures us. Because of it "Jesus has become the guarantee of a better covenant." "Better," as we have already seen, is a favorite word of the author. So is "covenant," which appears here the first of seventeen times in Hebrews. "Covenant" means "will" or "testament." God's covenant with man is entirely unilateral. It sets forth his will and is entirely his doing and comes completely from him. This "better covenant" of salvation will be discussed more fully later, but Jesus is its "guarantee."

Note the strategic use of his name "Jesus." Jesus the Savior with all that he has done is the guarantee of this better covenant. "Guarantee" is a word used only here in the New Testament and means about as much as "reliable security." A guarantee is some reliable security that what the covenant states will be carried out. What a glorious guarantee we have from God about his better covenant of salvation! It is Jesus who prepared that salvation, Jesus who stands as our priest forever, as sure as the sworn oath of an unchangeable God, Jesus who assures us into eternity that God will do for us exactly what he has promised.

[23]Now there have been many of those priests, since death prevented them from continuing in office; [24]but because Jesus lives forever, he has a permanent priesthood. [25]Therefore he is able to save completely those who come to God through him, because he always lives to intercede for them.

The author advances more proof of Christ's superiority as high priest. Once again he states, but in greater depth, the fact that Christ's priesthood is uninterrupted by death. One weakness of the Levitical priesthood as already pointed out in verses 8 and 16 was the mortality of those who held office. "There have been many of those priests." Josephus, a Jewish historian of the first century, even counted 83 of them from Aaron, its first high priest, to the last one serving when the temple was destroyed in A.D. 70.

This constant changing in the Levitical high priesthood revealed its weakness. But "Jesus lives forever." His life is "indestructible" as verse 16 has already declared. And that means "he has a permanent priesthood." There's no retirement or replacement, no career cut short by death or carried on by a successor, just Jesus our Savior there always as our permanent high priest. To the blessings he brings us there is no end; all the advantages he offers are ever in place. Who of those Hebrew Christians would want to leave him for Levi's mortal line? Who today would want to replace him with human priests as if the veil were sewn up again and mediators between God and man once again necessary?

There is an important conclusion to be drawn from Christ's unchanging priesthood. It's about the salvation he prepares as priest. "He is able to save completely," the author states. "Able to save" — that's what those Levitical priests could not do and yet that's what every sinner needs. This priest can and he saves "completely." It's not a half-way salvation or a sacrifice which needs repetition. Once for all he has done it on the altar of the cross with himself the victim and himself the priest.

When the author states, "He is able to save completely those who come to God through him," he is not limiting the scope of Christ's saving work as if he did it only for those who would believe. Rather he points out the role and necessity of faith. Also by speaking of "those who come to God" he shows that believers need no other mediator. They need no human "go-betweens" by which to approach God but can come boldly and confidently to a dear Father in heaven because of the work of this great priest. The avenue is ever open because this priest "always lives to intercede for them."

On that first Maundy Thursday Peter learned about this priest's concern for intercession. In Luke 22:32 he heard his

Savior say, "I have prayed for you, Simon, that your faith may not fail." On that same evening Jesus prayed for his followers of all times. In John 17:9 he told his Father, "I am not praying for the world, but for those you have given me, for they are yours."

In heaven that intercessory prayer continues without end. Hour after hour, day after day, if there be such things in heaven, the high priest supports and sustains us with his prayers. What more can this priest do? He's done it all, cleansing us by his blood, renewing us daily by his Spirit, interceding for us constantly before his Father, presenting us at last faultless before his throne.

[26]Such a high priest meets our need — one who is holy, blameless, pure, set apart from sinners, exalted above the heavens. [27]Unlike the other high priests, he does not need to offer sacrifices day after day, first for his own sins, and then for the sins of the people. He sacrificed for their sins once for all when he offered himself. [28]For the law appoints as high priests men who are weak; but the oath, which came after the law, appointed the son, who has been made perfect forever.

The author concludes this section on Christ's superiority by pointing to the better sacrifice which this perfectly qualified high priest has offered. What kind of high priest do sinners need? What kind is fully fitted for the task? The one we have! Though the author does not mention him by name, the readers know who is meant. It is Jesus, the high priest forever in the order of Melchizedek.

He is "holy" also according to his human nature. Not even the smallest speck of pollution can be found in him, not even the slightest deviation from God's commandments. To expound more fully on Christ's holiness, the author uses three synonymous statements. He is "blameless," doing no evil, having nothing base or bad attached to him. He is "pure," undefiled morally by anything that could hinder his high priestly work. And he is "set apart from sinners." Though he had to live among sinners, yet he never joined them in their sins. "A lamb without blemish or defect," Peter described him in 1 Peter 1:19. He was a priest who could challenge his enemies in John 8:46, "Can any of you prove me guilty of sin?" Also he is "exalted above the heavens." Since his ascension our high priest functions as our intercessor before the throne of God. What more can we need? *J*esus *E*xactly *S*erves *U*s *S*inners!

From Jesus' person the author turns to Jesus' work to show that he is the priest we need. He was not only the perfect priest, but also the perfect sacrifice. In 5:3 the author told us that the Levitical high priest on the yearly Day of Atonement had to make sacrifice for his own sins before he offered for the sins of the people. Now the thought is repeated and then contrasted with our high priest. Daily Jesus intercedes for sinners before his Father in heaven as that Old Testament high priest did once a year.

But our priest does not have to "day after day" first offer up for his own sins as that Levitical high priest had to do once a year on the Day of Atonement. What need does a "holy, blameless, pure, set apart from sinners" high priest have for sacrifices for himself ? This fact already marks him as eminently superior to the Levitical high priest.

So does the sacrifice which Christ brought. "He sacrificed for their sins once for all when he offered himself." For himself no sacrifice was needed; for sinners no more than one was necessary. When Christ offered up himself, he did what those Levitical high priests could never do. He made the absolutely perfect and complete sacrifice for the sins of the whole world, as the next chapters will clearly show.

The contrast is evident and proves beyond a doubt Christ's superiority. The Mosaic Law, which supported the Levitical priesthood, came in 1500 B.C. David's psalm with God's oath establishing Christ's priesthood came about 1000 B.C. and clearly supplanted the old priesthood. The law recognized the weaknesses of the priests whom it appointed and made provisions for sacrifices for their sins, too. The sinless Son whom God appointed by his oath "has been made perfect forever," that is, he has reached his appointed goal once for all. He as God's own Son, come to earth, has perfectly and forever fulfilled the work of the high priest. With his one offering for sins he has opened wide the way to a holy Father in heaven.

The author doesn't ask the question, but it hangs there in the air. Did the readers really want to go back to a high priesthood long ago discarded by God? To weak and frail human priests needing sacrifices as much as they did? To the intercession of high priests just as mortal as they? Did they really want to leave this superior high priest? Do we? For any reason? Lord, help it ever be,

> Jesus I will never leave,
> Who for me himself hath given;
> He redemption did achieve,
> Jesus I will never leave.

He Is a Priest Superior in Sanctuary and Covenant

8 **The point of what we are saying is this: We do have such a high priest, who sat down at the right hand of the throne of the Majesty in heaven, ²and who serves in the sanctuary, the true tabernacle set up by the Lord, not by man.**

Judaism was also quite concerned about the place where the priests served. The temple in the holy city with its outward splendor and ritualism stood impressively visible to their eyes and was etched vividly on their minds. Were those Hebrew Christians looking back in that direction and wavering? Then it was time to discuss the sanctuary in which the great high priest serves and point out also its superiority.

The author goes right to the point, stating at once the main thought of what is coming. "We do have such a high priest," he asserts, sounding a triumphant note. It's as if he is reminding the readers, "Look at the high priest we have. His sacrificial work on earth is finished and he occupies the position of all power and glory in heaven. What do the priests of Judaism look like compared to him?"

"Right hand of the throne" describes a position of highest power and glory while "Majesty in heaven" reverently refers to God. Our priest is an exalted royal one, not a limited, earthly one. He is in heaven with his work of sacrificing done, not busy on earth repeating sacrifices which can be nothing more than symbols.

Even more emphatically and clearly the author states that Christ "serves in the sanctuary, the true tabernacle set up by the Lord, not by man." The word "serves" catches our attention especially since it stands in sharp contrast to what we have just been told of Christ's exalted position in heaven. Coming from the same Greek word as the word "liturgy," it designates office holders of various kinds with the context helping to determine what service is to be rendered. The exalted Christ is busy serving as our priest in heaven.

The other words which catch our attention are the synonyms "sanctuary" and "tabernacle." Both take us back to Israel's wilderness days when they set up the special tent which was called the tabernacle and which symbolized the Lord's presence in their midst. That tent in the wilderness was sacred; so also was the glorious temple later in Jerusalem. But these were not the true dwelling place of God. Sinful men set them up and sinful priests served in them. Christ serves in the true tabernacle set up by the Lord. That tabernacle is heaven itself as Hebrews 9:24 explains, "For Christ did not enter a man-made sanctuary that was only a copy of the true one; he entered heaven itself, now to appear for us in God's presence." In heaven our high priest serves, representing believers and reigning forever.

3Every high priest is appointed to offer both gifts and sacrifices, and so it was necessary for this one also to have something to offer. 4If he were on earth, he would not be a priest, for there were already men who offer the gifts prescribed by the law. 5They serve at a sanctuary that is a copy and shadow of what is in heaven. This is why Moses was warned when he was about to build the tabernacle: "See to it that you make everything according to the pattern shown you on the mountain." 6But the ministry Jesus has received is as superior to theirs as the covenant of which he is mediator is superior to the old one, and it is founded on better promises.

Only a heavenly sanctuary would serve for this great high priest. The offering he brings quickly points this out. A significant function of the Levitical high priesthood was to "offer both gifts and sacrifices." Note that the author uses the plural "gifts and sacrifices" and also the present tense for the infinitive "to offer." This work of bringing gifts and sacrifices was never finished. Every year on the Day of Atonement the high priest had to repeat it.

Now look at Jesus our great high priest. He also had to have "something to offer," but there is a difference. In the Greek the form of the verb "to offer" used here is not in the present tense, as was the previous one, implying repeated and continuing sacrificing. Rather, the verb form used here suggests that he offered only once. This thought is reinforced when we see that the "something" he offered is in the singular, referring to an individual sacrifice.

Could the reader miss what was meant? Verse 27 in chapter 7 has already told us, "He sacrificed for their sins once for all when he offered himself," and chapter 9 will elaborate on this. Now in heaven's sanctuary the great high priest constantly uses this once-for-all sacrifice to plead the case of poor sinners. His sacrifice completed on Calvary's cross forms the sure basis for his continued service as priest interceding for sinners before his Father's throne.

Such a priest with such a sacrifice would not serve in the earthly tabernacle. Because the author writes as though the temple is still standing and the Levitical priesthood still functioning, we gather that the date was sometime before A.D. 70. Though Christ had rent the veil in the temple with his perfect sacrifice on Calvary and thus rendered the Old Testament priesthood obsolete, yet it continued till Rome's legions destroyed the temple in A.D. 70. In such a temple there was no room for someone from Judah to bring such a special sacrifice, only room for priests from Levi's line to bring the repeated offerings.

Our high priest must have a radically different sanctuary in which to serve. Did the readers realize how superior that heavenly sanctuary was? The author tells them by pointing out how the earthly tabernacle in the wilderness was a "copy and shadow of what is in heaven." "Copy" indicates some kind of sketch plan while "shadow" refers to some reflection or silhouette.

The words are plain. The tabernacle which God in Exodus 25:40 instructed Moses to build was only a shadow of what was shown him. The earthly tabernacle which the Jews prized highly was only a copy. The original was in heaven. Just as the Levitical priesthood was only a shadow of

Christ's priesthood, so the sanctuary in which it served was only a shadow of the heavenly one in which Christ functioned. The point has to be clear as to who was the superior high priest.

Christ's superiority is shown also by the covenant he mediated. In 7:22 he was called the "guarantee of a better covenant." Here, as also in 9:15 and 12:24, he is described as the "mediator," the middle-man who steps between two parties. "Covenant" again as in 7:22 is "will" or "testament." In Greek there are two words for "covenant." The more common word always involves two parties who can more or less bargain with each other as equals, such as with a marriage contract. The other word, used here, is one-sided as in a "will," where the one bequeathing says, "This is what I want to happen and this is the way it will be."

What is the "superior" covenant of which Christ is the mediator? It is God's bequest of salvation with the better promises of pardon and life put into force by the death of the Mediator. This "will," already promised to Abraham, was "founded" or given legal force when Jesus stepped into the gap between God and man on Calvary's cross.

Were the ears of those Jewish Christians perked up now? "Covenant" was an important word in Judaism and talk about a superior covenant with better promises than the treasured Mosaic one had to catch their attention.

7For if there had been nothing wrong with that first covenant, no place would have been sought for another. 8But God found fault with the people and said, "The time is coming, declares the Lord, when I will make a new covenant with the house of Israel and with the house of Judah. 9It will not be like the covenant I made with their forefathers when I took them by the hand to lead them out of Egypt, because they did not remain faithful to my covenant, and I turned away from them, declares the Lord. 10This is the covenant

I will make with the house of Israel after that time, declares the Lord. I will put my laws in their minds and write them on their hearts. I will be their God and they will be my people. [11]No longer will a man teach his neighbor, or a man his brother, saying, 'Know the Lord,' because they will all know me, from the least of them to the greatest. [12]For I will forgive their wickedness and will remember their sins no more." [13]By calling this covenant "new," he has made the first one obsolete and what is obsolete and aging will soon disappear.

The Jews highly prized the covenant which God had given through Moses at Mt. Sinai. For them it was the final and faultless word. In it they found laws governing their priesthood, temple rituals, sacrifices, holy days and the like. The Hebrew Christians under persecution's pressure were thinking of going back to Judaism with its Mosaic Covenant. Perhaps they had made a mistake in accepting Christianity; perhaps the old covenant was better.

The author has an answer for them: "If there had been nothing wrong with that first covenant, no place would have been sought for another." The old covenant was replaced, not because it was imperfect and riddled with flaws, but because it was inadequate and incomplete, only preparatory. God's covenant through Moses was basically law and as such had two deficiencies. It revealed sin, but could not remove it. It demanded perfect obedience, but could not give the power for it.

Certainly the Mosaic Covenant, besides the ceremonial and political laws, contained also the moral law, summarized in the Ten Commandments. This moral law stands for all time as shown in its being repeated in the New Testament, but law as Paul reminds us in Romans 8:3 is "powerless" and "weakened by the sinful nature." To regard the Mosaic Covenant as final instead of preparatory was to fall far short of the better promise God had in mind for his people.

God himself showed where the problem lay with the old covenant. He "found fault with the people." Exodus 19:8 and 24:7 record how when God gave his covenant through Moses, the people responded, "We will do everything the Lord has said." But they couldn't and didn't. How glaringly short they fell the author of Hebrews has already shown in chapter 3.

Though good and holy in itself, the old covenant was powerless to give obedience or life. So God himself replaced it with a better covenant. Already about 600 B.C. through his prophet Jeremiah he had declared that he would "make a new covenant with the house of Israel and with the house of Judah." "New" means more than just more recent. It means new in quality. "Make" means to bring to completion. When the eternal priest on Calvary's cross said, "It is finished," he completed the covenant which now stands in effect till Judgment Day.

Note well who is speaking and who is making the covenant. It is the "Lord," the God of grace who keeps his promises. Four times the words, "declares the Lord" appear in this quotation from Jeremiah 31. Again and again in that quotation God declares, "I will make," "I will put," "I will be," "I will forgive."

With "house of Israel" and "house of Judah" God was referring to New Testament Israel. The nation of Israel at Jeremiah's time was already gone, lost in captivity among the Assyrians. The nation of Judah in 588 B.C. would disappear into the 70-year Babylonian captivity. Though Judah reappeared briefly so that the Christ Child could be born of them as promised, yet the time came in A.D. 70 when Judah was dispersed. Already in Jeremiah's day God referred to a different Israel and Judah, to the spiritual descendants of Abraham, to the believers "from every nation, tribe, people and language" as described in Revelation 7:9.

"New in quality," God had said of his replacement covenant. It would not be conditional like the one given through Moses at Sinai. God's love and mercy had been evident then, too. Like some loving father he had taken Israel by the hand, leading and supporting the people with tender concern. But Israel ended up abandoning the covenant and God "turned away," stopping his care for them. What else could he do? He could not bestow blessings on those who disregarded his covenant and disobeyed its precepts. The old covenant failed because it could not produce the obedience it required. The new covenant could not fail because it was pure gospel and unconditional grace.

"Better promises" the author had said of this replacement covenant. Now he explains. Promise number one quotes from Jeremiah 31:33, "I will put my laws in their minds and write them on their hearts." There would be no need for those two inscribed stone tablets, no more struggling to obey because of fear. God's people under the new covenant of grace will have his laws written on their minds and hearts. The law will be a part of their inner being. With their minds they will know and with their hearts love what God wants. The compulsion to obey will come not from without, but from within, from a heart of faith that responds with the Psalmist as in Psalm 119:32, "I run in the path of your commands, for you have set my heart free." This is regeneration. The new covenant produces a heart of faith which has not only knowledge of, but also power for walking in God's ways.

Promise number two quotes also Jeremiah 31:33, "I will be their God, and they will be my people." Those who have been to Calvary are the people of God in a most special way. Liberty, security, eternity are theirs as surely as his promise, "I am yours and you are mine." They are "God's possession" as Ephesians 1:14 describes them, connected to him by an unbreakable blood-bought bond. Believers are "no longer foreigners and aliens, but fellow citizens with God's people and members of God's household" as Ephesians 2:19 so gloriously describes them.

Promise number three repeats the words of Jeremiah 31:34. Under the old covenant there was constant need for knowledge. Prophet after prophet appeared to reveal increasingly more of God's will. Both "neighbors" in the wider community and "brothers" in the narrower family circle had to be taught. Still man's knowledge and God's revelation were incomplete. In the new covenant of grace every believer will know God. The Son will reveal and the Spirit will record so that believers will have intimate knowledge of the God of their salvation. Better indeed! Just think of knowing him like Abraham, to whom God told his secrets, or like Moses, with whom God spoke face to face, or like Mary, whose tears he dried on Easter, or like John the Divine, to whom he gave those glorious revelations. In the new covenant all believers will have that blessed privilege, "from the least of them to the greatest."

Promise number four continues the quote from Jeremiah 31:34, "For I will forgive their wickedness and will remember their sins no more." Their wickedness with its resulting guilt God will forgive. Not that he ignores or overlooks it. God forgives it because he has dealt with it through the atoning sacrifice of his Son. Nor does he keep files or dredge up sins sporadically from the past. He wipes them completely from his memory by the blood of his Son. They are forgiven and forgotten by the God of all grace. He removes our transgressions from us "as far as the east is from the west" (Psalm 103:12) and "hurl[s] all our iniquities into the depths of the sea" (Micah 7:19). When God says, "I will forgive" and "I will remember no more," the believing sinner can be sure. "Therefore, there is now no condemnation for those who are in Christ Jesus" (Romans 8:1).

Better promises? Indeed! A new covenant of superior quality? Who could doubt it? Jeremiah had already foretold it about 600 B.C.; Jesus had put it into force about A.D. 33. Soon the old covenant weakened and tottering like some senile aged person would completely disappear. After General Titus' Roman legions in A.D. 70 finished with Jerusalem, there was no more sanctuary or priesthood, and there were no more sacrifices. But the new covenant, the one established by a gracious God and founded on the better promises of salvation, stands. Under its scope God deals with us as his children, till we enter the Jerusalem above, where the clouds of sin never again darken the skies and where we shall know the God of all grace as fully as he knows us.

He Is a Priest Superior in Sacrifice

9 Now the first covenant had regulations for worship and also an earthly sanctuary. ²A tabernacle was set up. In its first room were the lampstand, the table and the consecrated bread; this was called the Holy Place. ³Behind the second curtain was a room called the Most Holy Place, ⁴which had the golden altar of incense and the gold-covered ark of the covenant. This ark contained the gold jar of manna, Aaron's staff that had budded, and the stone tablets of the covenant. ⁵Above the ark were the cherubim of the Glory, overshadowing the atonement cover. But we cannot discuss these things in detail now.

Christ's superior priesthood is still the subject under discussion. Nothing points out that superiority more than the sacrifice involved, as the author now shows. Since sacrifice required also a place for it, the author takes his readers back to the Tabernacle. This sacred tent, which served the Jews in the wilderness, was the model for the temples later erected in Jerusalem. God himself had given the pattern for the Tabernacle (8:5) and also the regulations governing the worship conducted in it. The Tabernacle was important in its day and the author writes about it with respect, but it was only "earthly." It was built by man and only of this world's scene.

The reader would do well to turn to chapters 25-40 of the Old Testament book of Exodus for background information about the Tabernacle. The tent was 30 cubits by 10 cubits by 10 cubits. With the cubit being about 18 inches, the distance from the elbow to the tip of the middle finger, this translates into 45 feet long, 15 feet wide, and 15 feet high.

The Tabernacle was divided into two parts. The first room was the Holy Place with a length of 30 feet and a curtain screening off its entrance. Behind it was the second room, fifteen feet long, called the Most Holy Place. This, too, had a curtain shutting it off, an elaborate one woven of blue, purple and scarlet wool and finely twisted linen and decorated with the figures of cherubim.

In the first room stood the "lampstand," the golden candelabrum with its seven oil lamps to furnish light in the windowless tent. Also in the first room was the "table," constructed of wood covered with gold, on which was laid the "consecrated bread." From Leviticus 24:5-9 we learn there were twelve cakes, one for each of the twelve tribes of Israel, baked of fine, unleavened flour, changed every Sabbath, with the old loaves to be eaten by the priests only. These loaves were also called the "bread of the Presence" since they were set before the presence of God.

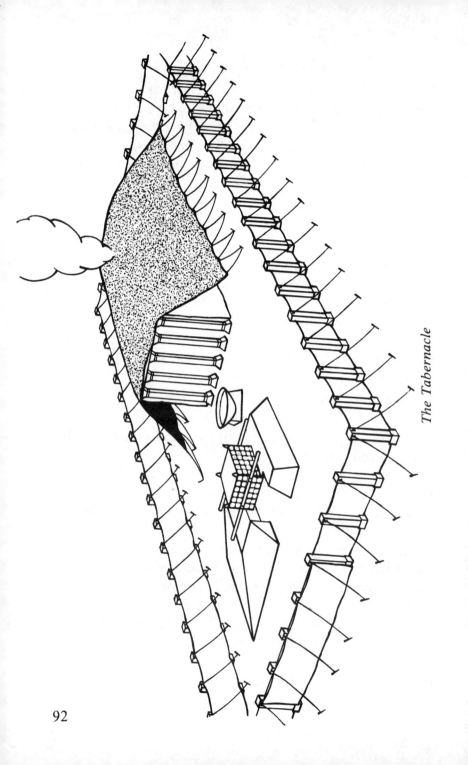

The Tabernacle

The Ark of the Covenant

Also in the Holy Place stood the "golden altar of incense." Exodus 30:6 explains that this altar stood "in front of the curtain" which closed off the Most Holy Place. From Leviticus 16:12,13 we learn that on the Day of Atonement the high priest carried burning incense from this altar behind the curtain into the Most Holy Place so that its smoke would cover the mercy seat and protect him from death. Because of these facts the author connects the golden altar of incense with the Most Holy Place.

In the Most Holy Place stood only one item, "the gold-covered ark of the covenant." Exodus 25:10-22 describes this box as 2½ cubits long, 1½ cubits high and 1½ cubits wide, covered inside and out with gold. Two cherubim of hammered gold stood on its cover, one on each end. "Cherubim of the Glory" the author calls them because God was present in his glory between them. Scripture especially connects the cherubim with God's presence as in Psalm 80:1. In Exodus 25:22 God said of the mercy seat, which the outstretched wings of those two cherubim overshadowed, "There . . . I will meet with you." The lid of the ark was called "the atonement cover." On this golden top between the two cherubim the high priest on the Day of Atonement sprinkled the sacrificial blood to symbolize sin's atonement.

Inside the ark was the "jar of manna" of which Exodus 16:32-34 spoke, though here the author adds under inspiration the detail that it was a "gold" jar. Also inside was "Aaron's staff" which God, as recorded in Numbers 17:1-11, had caused to bud and yield almonds and thus had proven Moses' leadership before rebellious Israel. And inside were "the stone tablets of the covenant" which God in Exodus 25:16 had commanded Moses to put into this most sacred place.

Both the gold jar of manna and Aaron's rod were gone from the ark by Solomon's time (1 Kings 8:9), perhaps lost when the Philistines had captured it (1 Samuel 4:10,11). The stone tablets and the ark itself disappeared later, perhaps when Nebuchadnezzar set fire to the temple (2 Kings 25:8,9).

Much more could have been said about this sacred tent and its special items, but this brief mention was enough. The author wanted to stress, not these earthly types, but the superior high priest and his very special sacrifice to which they pointed.

6 When everything had been arranged like this, the priests entered regularly into the outer room to carry on their ministry. 7But only the high priest entered the inner room, and that only once a year, and never without blood, which he offered for himself and for the sins the people had committed in ignorance. 8The Holy Spirit was showing by this that the way into the Most Holy Place had not yet been disclosed as long as the first tabernacle was still standing. 9This is an illustration for the present time, indicating that the gifts and sacrifices being offered were not able to clear the conscience of the worshiper. 10They are only a matter of food and drink and various ceremonial washings — external regulations applying until the time of the new order.

With Christ's superior sacrifice in mind, the author proceeds to elaborate on what went on in the Tabernacle. Into the first room the common priests entered regularly. Twice daily they went in to offer incense on the golden altar, both in the morning and the evening (Exodus 30:1-8) while at the same time tending the oil lamps. Their service also included changing the consecrated bread every Sabbath Day (Leviticus 24:5-8). Already here we find restrictions. Not the people, but only the priests could pass through the outer curtain into this first room of the Tabernacle.

Restrictions become even more apparent as the author proceeds to what went on behind the second curtain in that special room called the Most Holy Place. That room was entered only on one day during the year and only by the high priest and never without blood. The author refers to the Day of Atonement, the most important day of Israel's religious year, and the most important sacrifice which was brought on that day. If he can show Christ's sacrifice to be superior to that of the high priest on that day, he has made his point.

In 5:2,3 we have already seen how on that day the high priest entered into the Most Holy Place first with sacrificial blood for his own sins and then a second time with blood for the sins which the people had committed in ignorance. To enter within those sacred precincts without blood would have meant death, even for the high priest.

All these restrictions, all this blood, indeed, the very pattern of the Tabernacle itself, involved deep religious truth. The Holy Spirit, the divine Revealer of truth, was showing that sin's impenetrable curtain had sealed off man's access to the holy God, that God could be approached only through a mediator, and that this mediator could draw near only with the blood of a sacrifice. The existence of this Tabernacle symbolized that entrance into God's Most Holy Place of heaven was impossible for sinful man. Viewed against this background, how significant the rending of the temple curtain at Christ's crucifixion becomes.

The Tabernacle with its entrance restrictions and endless rituals illustrated something else. "For the present time," that is for the Old Testament time during which they existed, the Tabernacle with its rituals effected only external cleansing. This "present time" could also include the transitional period in which the author and his readers were living (up to the time of the temple's destruction in A.D. 70). At that time ceremonial laws were still being observed on a voluntary basis, but the repeated "gifts and sacrifices" could not take care of the worshiper's real need. They could make him ceremonially clean on the outside, but could not cleanse his conscience.

All those strict regulations about which food and drink could be used and which ceremonial washings needed to be performed were only "external" or fleshly. They applied only to the troubled sinner's body, not his conscience and were to last only until the "time of the new order." Yes, they prefigured spiritual truths and thus were valuable. They served as shadows of the coming great high priest who with his superior offering would completely cleanse the sinner's conscience. But now that the "time of the new order" is here, now that Christ has ushered in the glorious New Testament period with his crib and cross, what need is there any longer for illustrative tabernacles and external regulations?

11When Christ came as high priest of the good things that are already here, he went through the greater and more perfect tabernacle that is not man-made, that is to say, not a part of this creation. 12He did not enter by means of the blood of goats and calves; but he entered the Most Holy Place once for all by his own blood, having obtained eternal redemption. 13The blood of goats and bulls and the ashes of a heifer sprinkled on those who are ceremonially unclean sanctify them so that they are outwardly clean. 14How much more, then, will the blood of Christ, who through the eternal Spirit offered himself unblemished to God, cleanse our consciences from acts that lead to death so that we may serve the living God!

Now comes the contrast — and how sharp it is. First the author shows the superiority of the tabernacle in which Christ our high priest serves. It is not "man-made," not constructed by men of earthly materials like the Jewish Tabernacle. It is not even "part of this creation," not coming from God's creative hand like the heavens and the earth. It is the eternal heaven where the eternal God dwells. No wonder the author describes it as a "greater and more perfect tabernacle."

In the eternal presence of God Christ dwells because he had come as "the high priest of the good things that are already here." Note his title "Christ" or "Anointed" is used to remind us of his office. He had come to earth to function as high priest and thereby to secure "good things" for us. Because of his sacrificial work on the cross the good blessings of salvation and all that goes with it are ours already to enjoy. What a contrast — our priest serves in a heavenly tabernacle.

The next contrast is just as vivid. Look at the offering he brought. Yes, it was "blood" just as with Israel's high priests. Blood was important in their sacrifices, as Leviticus 17:11 points out, because blood was a vivid reminder that God demanded death for sin. Unlike the high priests, Christ did not bring the blood of goats and calves, but his own blood, holy and precious because it was the blood of the God-man. So he did not have to come year after year with his blood as the high priest had to. "Once and for all" he offered and thereby achieved "eternal redemption." To redeem means to set free by paying the price. Forever in heaven Christ points to his blood as having freed us from all sin and guilt.

The contrast in offerings is sharpened by pointing to their effects. Outward cleanliness for people ceremonially unclean was all that the blood of goats and bulls could offer. The reference to the sprinkling by "the ashes of a heifer" particularly points out this limitation. In Numbers 19 God made provision for cleansing those who would become ceremonially unclean by contact with dead bodies, human bones, or graves. Such unclean people were to be sprinkled with water into which the ashes of a sacrificial heifer had been mixed. Outward defilement was involved so outward cleansing was offered. But that was all! These sacrifices did nothing to get rid of sin's more serious defilement of the soul.

Now the author bids us look more closely at Christ's offering. The animals which the priests offered had nothing to say in the matter and did not even know what was going on. Christ offered himself willingly. With him went the "eternal Spirit" guiding and encouraging him along the way in this awesome task just as God had promised. In Isaiah 42:1 God had said of his willing servant, "I will put my Spirit on him."

Besides being a voluntary sacrifice, Christ was also an "unblemished" one. God's demand that the Old Testament sacrificial animals be free of all physical defects pointed to his spotless, sinless Son, who would lay himself on the altar of the cross.

And the results of this perfect sacrifice? His blood reaches far beyond the skin and produces more than outward cleanness. It "cleanse[s] our consciences from acts that lead to death, so that we may serve the living God." All the works of natural man are done in spiritual death and can only lead to eternal death. For him there is no peace, only the frantic rubbing of his conscience with the abrasive steel wool of worthless works. But for us, peace washes over the conscience when by the Spirit we behold our heavenly Sacrifice and believe "by his wounds we are healed" (Isaiah 53:5). Then loving service to a living God can and will follow in daily life.

¹⁵For this reason Christ is the mediator of a new covenant, that those who are called may receive the promised eternal inheritance — now that he has died as a ransom to set them free from the sins committed under the first covenant. ¹⁶In the case of a will, it is necessary to prove the death of the one who made it, ¹⁷because a

will is in force only when somebody has died; it never takes effect while the one who made it is living. [18]This is why even the first covenant was not put into effect without blood. [19] When Moses had proclaimed every commandment of the law to all the people, he took the blood of calves, together with water, scarlet wool and branches of hyssop, and sprinkled the scroll and all the people. [20]He said, "This is the blood of the covenant, which God has commanded you to keep." [21]In the same way, he sprinkled with the blood both the tabernacle and everything used in its ceremonies. [22]In fact, the law requires that nearly everything be cleansed with blood, and without the shedding of blood there is no forgiveness.

How absolutely essential Christ's sacrifice was. Without it there would be no new covenant in force and no eternal inheritance for anyone. That is the thought the author next sets forth. "For this reason Christ is the mediator of a new covenant," he writes, "that those who are called may receive the promised eternal inheritance — now that he has died as a ransom to set them free from the sins committed under the first covenant." The author is not limiting the effects of Christ's redemption to those who lived under and sinned against the Mosaic covenant. Christ's death covers all sinners, past, present, and future.

But the author points out that Christ did what the old covenant of the law could not do. With his sacrificial death he mediated the new covenant of grace. He stepped between sinless God and sinful man and put God's covenant of salvation into force. Now "those who are called" to faith by God's gospel grace receive "the promised eternal inheritance." Whether they live before or after Calvary makes no difference. As heirs named in God's will, they receive his eternal inheritance, made sure by Christ's complete sacrifice.

With earthly wills and inheritances death is always necessary. It is a general principle that, as long as a man lives, the provisions of his last will and testament do not go into effect. He may have that will drawn up for years and locked securely away, but it does not go into effect till he dies. Then, when evidence has been produced of the testator's death, the heirs receive their inheritance.

Can we miss the author's point? Christ is both Testator and Mediator of the new covenant of salvation. As the "heir of all things" (1:2) he has also the eternal inheritance in his hands and wills it to us. As the Mediator he steps onto the cross and with his death puts this blessed testament into effect. Should the cross be a thing of dismay for anyone? Should blood theology make us squirm? Without Christ's cross and blood we have nothing to inherit.

Apparently the Jewish Christians to whom the author was writing were questioning the necessity of Christ's death. The author has already answered by reminding them that wills and inheritances involve death. Now he answers by urging them to look back at the old covenant. Had they forgotten how much blood was involved in that Mosaic covenant? Didn't they remember how "the first covenant was not put into effect without blood"? From its very inception the Mosaic covenant operated with sacrificial blood.

To show this, the author went back to Exodus 24:1-8, even adding some details under the inspiration of the Spirit. When God gave the old covenant at Mt. Sinai, Moses first proclaimed all its requirements to the people so that everyone understood. Then he took sacrificial blood, extended in quantity with water, and with a sponge of hyssop, wrapped with scarlet wool, sprinkled it on "the scroll and all the people." "This is the blood of the covenant, which God commanded you to keep," he told them. The blood, when sprinkled on the scroll, put the Mosaic covenant into effect. When sprinkled on the people, it bound them to the regulations of the covenant and promised blessings for obedience.

Later when the Tabernacle was built, blood was used again. Moses sprinkled it both on the Tabernacle and on the sacred vessels used in the religious ceremonies. Though Exodus 40:9 in recording this event mentions only the sprinkling with oil, the author of Hebrews under divine inspiration adds the detail that blood was also used.

Who could miss the symbolism? Blood was necessary. "In fact, the law requires that nearly everything be cleansed with blood," as those Jewish readers should have well remembered from their Old Testament Scriptures. The Mosaic law demanded bloody sacrifices for sin offerings. Only the very poor as outlined in Leviticus 5:11 could bring four pints of flour as a substitute for blood.

To emphasize, the author repeats the thought, "Without the shedding of blood there is no forgiveness." All the animal blood connected with the old covenant reminded Israel that they and everything they touched were sinful and needed cleansing. Even more important, all that blood pointed ahead to the greatest sacrifice ever, the pouring out of the blood of God's Son which alone can remove sin's spots and stains. Well do Christians love to sing of this blood!

23It was necessary, then, for the copies of the heavenly things to be purified with these sacrifices, but the heavenly things themselves with better sacrifices than these. 24For Christ did not enter a man-made sanctuary that was only a copy of the true one; he entered heaven itself, now to appear for us in God's presence. 25Nor did he enter heaven to offer himself again and again, the way the high priest enters the Most Holy Place every year with blood that is not his own. 26Then Christ would have had to suffer many

times since the creation of the world. **But now he has appeared once for all at the end of the ages to do away with sin by the sacrifice of himself.** [27]**Just as man is destined to die once, and after that to face judgment,** [28]**so Christ was sacrificed once to take away the sins of many people; and he will appear a second time, not to bear sin, but to bring salvation to those who are waiting for him.**

Now again comes the contrast — and again note how sharp it is. If earthly things like tabernacles and equipment needed purifying with sacrifices, how about the heavenly which they copied? Would they not require "better sacrifices" than the blood of animals? This verse has caused considerable concern for commentators. The plural used in "better sacrifices" has troubled some since obviously Christ's once-for-all sacrifice must be meant. A simple explanation is that the plural is used because the statement is general in form, contrasting not many versus one sacrifice, but lesser versus greater.

More troubling is the question about the purifying of the "heavenly things." What are these heavenly things and what kind of purifying is meant? Heaven where God dwells is perfect as he is and needs no cleansing. But a cleansing is needed as heaven is entered by sinful man.

The cleansing blood of Christ enables sinners to enter into and enjoy "the heavenly things" without defiling them. This blood ushers sinners into heaven, all the while keeping heaven free of their sin and its consequences. The believer's entrance into the heavenly presence of God begins already here on earth the moment he's brought to faith. Christ's cross is stamped indelibly on that entrance for only his sacrifice makes this blessed communion with God possible for sinners. When sin, as it still clings to the believer, threatens to disrupt that fellowship, again only Christ's sacrifice avails.

In heaven Christ "appears for us in God's presence." No earthly priest is he, standing before a gold-covered ark in some man-made sanctuary smoky with incense. Our high priest stands in the very presence of God, not to look upon him, but to be looked upon by him as the accepted sacrifice for sin. There he pleads "for us" and always successfully. His blood shed on earth has already paid our penalty and won for us God's acquittal. What need is there for such a perfect sacrifice to be repeated?

The high priests of Judaism would have been content to sacrifice only once, but their sacrifices had to be repeated. This priest's sacrifice counted "once and for all" for sins from Adam and Eve on down. When he appeared at "the end of the ages," all history came into focus. To his cross with its sacrifice all past ages were leading; by his cross all present and future ones are guided. Those Hebrew Christians were living in this glorious New Testament time. They knew how Christ had done away with sin, canceling its guilt and cracking its grip. How could they even think of turning away from such a Savior? To believe what he had done would mean to rejoice all the day through.

Once more the author presents Christ's perfect sacrifice, this time from another perspective. "Man is destined to die once." It is a circumstance of life over which man has no control and which, though he try to forget, he cannot avoid. And death is serious because judgment follows. At death's moment God's verdict is pronounced — with the soul going either to heaven or to hell, to be followed on the Last Day by his body. Now consider our great high priest. He did not merely die; he was sacrificed, but only once, and that was enough to satisfy God's judgment. By that sacrifice the sins of all, whom the author describes as "many" in contrast to the One who bore those sins, were canceled.

But Calvary with its cross is not the end of redemption's story. Nor is the scene in heaven's Most Holy Place where the ascended priest represents his people. The final chapter remains to be written. When Christ returns to earth, he won't be concerned about sin. Oh yes, he will have something to say to unbelievers about their sins, and for a million worlds none of us would want to be in their shoes. But for those "who are waiting for him," holding out eagerly for that great Last Day, his return will bring full enjoyment of salvation. The apostle's words in 1 John 3:2 mirror our thoughts: "Dear friends, now we are children of God, and what we will be has not yet been made known. But we know that when he appears, we shall be like him, for we shall see him as he is." How we wait for his return!

10 **The law is only a shadow of the good things that are coming — not the realities themselves. For this reason it can never, by the same sacrifices repeated endlessly year after year, make perfect those who draw near to worship. ²If it could would they not have stopped being offered? For the worshipers would have been cleansed once for all, and would no longer have felt guilty for their sins. ³But those sacrifices are an annual reminder of sins, ⁴because it is impossible for the blood of bulls and goats to take away sins.**

Do we get the feeling that the author has been somewhat repeating himself? Yes, indeed, purposely so! Throughout this first part of his letter, the theme has been "What a supreme treasure we have in Christ." No more glorious theme could be found; his readers were to be perfectly clear about this truth. So as the author draws this doctrinal portion of his letter to a close, he once more repeats and reinforces the thought of the superior Christ and his all-sufficient sacrifice for sin. Note how he ends each of the brief sections with a reference to that perfect sacrifice.

Once more the author takes his readers back to the Old Testament law with its commands about the sacrificial system. How inadequate it was. In dismissal the author summarizes the law as only a shadow of the good things to come. Shadows are not "the realities themselves," but only vague previews of what is coming. Those animal sacrifices only hinted at the "good things" of salvation which Christ's real sacrifice would bring. To turn back now from Christ to the shadow would be like preferring a photo to the real person. What an insult that would be!

Because those sacrifices were only shadows, they needed to be "repeated endlessly year after year." Every year for centuries the ritual on the Day of Atonement was the same. Yet repetition did not bring remission of sin. Animal sacrifices made no one "perfect." They brought no one to the goal of forgiveness of sin and fellowship with God. If they had, why were those sacrifices repeated endlessly? If surgery is successful, it need not be repeated over and over. If cleansing for the guilty conscience is there, additional cleansing need not be obtained.

Those repeated sacrifices did not soothe the sinner's conscience, but rather stabbed it awake each year. Instead of erasing the sinner's guilt, the annual sacrifices emphasized it. The conclusion was obvious, "It is impossible for the blood of bulls and goats to take away sins." "Take away" means to remove something so completely that it is no longer in the picture. That's what man needed done with his sins, and that's what animal blood was incapable of doing. To try removing sin with animal blood was as futile as attempting to build a mountain to the moon with teaspoonfuls of sand. Could the readers miss the author's emphasis? "Don't look back at those Old Testament sacrifices," he was saying. "They couldn't remove even a speck of sin's guilt, but only pointed ahead to Christ whose perfect sacrifice would remove it all. LOOK AT HIM!"

⁵Therefore, when Christ came into the world, he said: "Sacrifice and offering you did not desire, but a body you prepared for me; ⁶with burnt offerings and sin offerings you were not pleased. ⁷Then I said, 'Here I am — it is written about me in the scroll — I have come to do your will, O God.'"⁸First he said, "Sacrifices and offerings, burnt offerings and sin offerings you did not desire, nor were you pleased with them" (although the law required them to be made). ⁹Then he said, "Here I am, I have come to do your will." He sets aside the first to establish the second. ¹⁰And by that will, we have been made holy through the sacrifice of the body of Jesus Christ once for all.

Again we see how the author uses the Old Testament Scriptures to prove his point. Again we have to marvel at how he under the Spirit's guidance sees Christ in that Old Testament. This time he quotes Psalm 40:6-8, used only here in the New Testament. In those words of David the author heard the Messiah, great David's greater Son, speaking. It's a beautiful conversation which the Son carried on with the Father.

"When Christ came into the world," refers to his entire incarnation and describes his constant attitude toward his Father during that time. Repeating the words for emphasis, the Messiah points out clearly what the Father did not desire. Sacrifices of any kind — whether animal "sacrifices" or meat and drink "offerings," whether voluntary "burnt offerings" which thankful people brought to the Tabernacle or the required "sin offerings" — were not what the Father desired. Rivers of animal blood and mountains of animal carcasses were not what God really wanted, though he had commanded them in the law. Also God could not be pleased with just the outward repetition of such sacrifices if willing,

It Is Finished

obedient hearts were not behind them. What God desired was that to which all those Old Testament sacrifices pointed, the willing sacrifice of his Son.

"A body you prepared for me" refers to this willing sacrifice. The footnote in your NIV Bible indicates that the author favors the Septuagint translation of Psalm 40:6. In the Hebrew it reads, "My ears you have pierced," referring to ears opened and made responsive to God's will, while the Septuagint paraphrases the thought to a body prepared to follow God's will. However we translate, the thought is the same — a Messiah lovingly, obediently, perfectly following the Father's will, a Messiah who says, "Here I am — it is written about me in the scroll — I have come to do your will, O God." Wherever we unroll the Old Testament scroll, we find reference to the Son's wholehearted delight in carrying out his Father's will. God's will was that his Son make full and final sacrifice for sin and the Son's will perfectly agreed.

In one of our Lenten hymns we have the flavor of this heavenly conversation beautifully captured: " 'Go forth, my Son,' the Father saith, 'and free men from the fear of death, from guilt and condemnation. The wrath and stripes are hard to bear, but by thy passion men shall share the fruit of thy salvation.' " 'Yea, Father, yea, most willingly I'll bear what thou commandest; my will conforms to thy decree, I do what thou demandest.' O wondrous Love, what has thou done! The Father offers up his Son! The Son content, descendeth!"

Could those Jewish Christians miss the point? This quotation from David's psalm with the heavenly conversation it contained emphatically showed that Christ "sets aside the first to establish the second." The Levitical sacrifices have been abolished. Christ's sacrifice, willed by the Father and agreed to by the Son, has taken their place. To go back to what has been abolished or even to claim equal place for it would be eternal folly. It is Christ's sacrifice for sin or nothing.

With a compact summary again referring to Christ's sacrifice and its effects the author ends this paragraph. Once more he refers to God's "will," which Christ came to do and which is described as "the sacrifice of the body of Jesus Christ once for all." Earlier he had described Christ's sacrifice as "himself" and "his blood." Here it is his "body," because the same word was used in verse five and also because the shedding of blood involved the body in the sacrifice.

As in 7:27 he describes this willing sacrifice as "once for all," valid for all time with no repetition necessary or possible. And the blessed results? "We have been made holy," he says. Those whom God brings to faith are spotless in his eyes. Not one shred of contamination clings to them, not one ounce of condemnation weighs upon them. They are the "saints" of whom the New Testament speaks. "But," the author reminds his readers, "such an exalted position comes only through Christ's sacrifice. LOOK AT HIM!"

¹¹Day after day every priest stands and performs his religious duties; again and again he offers the same sacrifices, which can never take away sins. ¹²But when this priest had offered for all time one sacrifice for sins, he sat down at the right hand of God. ¹³Since that time he waits for his enemies to be made his footstool, ¹⁴because by one sacrifice he has made perfect forever those who are being made holy.

Again the author stresses the finality of Christ's perfect sacrifice for sin. The old covenant had an unending round of sacrifices which left sin untouched and consciences unrelieved. Not only did the high priest have to bring the same offering year after year on the Day of Atonement, so did the common priests day after day. Every morning and evening, as Numbers 28:3-8 relates, the common priest, assigned to that task for the day, was to offer a one-year-old unblemished male lamb, along with a grain offering of $1/10$ ephah of fine flour, mixed with $1/4$ hin of olive oil, plus a drink offering of $1/4$ hin of wine. Twice a day the priest stood there, day after day, with the same sacrifices. What clearer indication could there be that such sacrifices could "never take away sin" ? Animal blood and grain offerings were unable to strip away sin's guilt which like a cloak had wrapped itself around the sinner.

Israel's priests stood constantly at work bringing the same sacrifices and yet never removing sin. In sharp contrast, our high priest "offered for all time one sacrifice for sins" and with that one sacrifice totally effective "sat down at the right hand of God." The author has come full circle. Back in 1:3 he had already written, "After he (the Son) had provided purification for sins, he sat down at the right hand of the Majesty in heaven." Now he repeats this glorious thought.

In heaven in all glory and honor our high priest, whose perfect sacrifice was laid on the altar of the cross, now points to that completed sacrifice as the basis for his pleading for us when we sin. Romans 8:34 shows the sequence, "Who is he that condemns? Christ Jesus, who died — more than that, who was raised to life — is at the right hand of God and is also interceding for us." With the ascended Savior as our lawyer, the believer's case in heaven's court is eternally secure.

Let his enemies, though, be warned. The Lord is waiting for the time when all who oppose him will be "made his footstool." On that Last Day, as described in Philippians 2:10,11, every knee will bow before him and every tongue will confess that he is Lord. Who would want to stand at that day among his enemies quaking with abject fear because of his splendor and because of the horrible awareness of having rejected their only Savior?

Once more the author emphasizes, "By one sacrifice he has made perfect forever those who are being made holy." "Made perfect" he writes this time, using one of his favorite words. In 2:10, 5:9, 10:14, 11:40, 12:23 he uses the verb. In 6:1, 7:11, 12:2 it is the noun and in 9:11 the adjective, always with the thought of completeness in mind. In this verse it is the thought of man being brought to the completeness which God had in mind for him. Peace and pardon, harmony and heaven were God's goal for man. Believers or, as the author calls them, "Those who are being made holy" have been brought to this blessed goal. The present tense "are being made holy" reminds us how one after the other the Spirit through the gospel sets men free from sin and for service to their loving God. "But," the author again reminds his readers, "the goal of holiness comes only through Christ's sacrifice. LOOK AT HIM!"

[15]The Holy Spirit also testifies to us about this. First he says: [16]"This is the covenant I will make with them after that time, says the Lord. I will put my laws in their hearts, and I will write them on their minds." [17]Then he adds: "Their sins and lawless acts I will remember no more." [18]And where these have been forgiven, there is no longer any sacrifice for sin.

Another witness to the finality of Christ's perfect sacrifice is the Holy Spirit. He "also testifies to us about this," the author writes. Note the present tense "testifies," reminding us that the Spirit not only authored what was written in the past but also witnesses through it in the present. So also with the quotation from Jeremiah 31. Earlier in chapter 8 the author under the Spirit's guidance had quoted Jeremiah 31:31-34 to establish that God would replace the old covenant with a new one. Here only verses 33 and 34 are used, in abbreviated and modified form, to show that the main theme in that new covenant would be complete remission of sins. The new covenant involved an inward change of man. His heart would be regenerated so that it would know and willingly follow God's law.

But above all, in that new covenant man's sins and violations of God's laws would be completely removed. "I will remember them no more," God promised. God's holy justice does not practice selective memory so that only some sins are recalled, nor does it suffer from amnesia so that other sins are forgotten. God's justice sees all sins and demands that every one of them be punished. And that is what God's love and mercy did through Christ. With Christ's body broken and Christ's blood shed on the cross God's love paid for all sin. Such is the cause of God's blessed forgetfulness of our sins. So the Spirit testified already in the Old Testament and constantly does in the New.

Again we have that concluding reference to Christ's perfect sacrifice. "And where these have been forgiven, there is no longer any sacrifice for sin." When God has totally sent away our sins, when he has forgiven and forgotten them, because of Jesus' perfect sacrifice, why talk any more about or look for additional sacrifice for sin? Let the talk be about hearts appreciating that perfect sacrifice, lives offered to him in grateful praise, and efforts rekindled to spreading it to others. Let the motto be for us as for the author and his first readers, "We don't need anything else for salvation. Christ is our perfect Savior. LOOK AT HIM."

If we have no conviction of sin, this doctrinal portion of Hebrews will have meant little to us. He whose shoulders feel no weight seeks no relief, nor do healthy-feeling men look for a doctor. But if sin is something real to us, if the skeletons of past sins rattle in the closet of our conscience, if each night on our pillow the day passes in rather sordid review in spite of our best efforts, if we have ripped off the tinfoil from our inner being and recoiled at what we found there, then the walk through Hebrews 1:1-10:18 will have been a blessed experience for us. Then we'll agree WHAT A SUPREME TREASURE WE HAVE IN CHRIST!

PART TWO

WHAT WE ARE TO DO WITH THIS SUPREME TREASURE (10:19-13:25)

Let Us Draw Near to God in Confident Faith

[19] Therefore, brothers, since we have confidence to enter the Most Holy Place by the blood of Jesus, [20] by a new and living way opened for us through the curtain, that is, his body, [21] and since we have a great priest over the house of God,

With the preceding section the author of Hebrews has shown himself to be one of the deepest theologians of the New Testament. In the following section he shows himself also to be a concerned and able pastor. It is a section as vibrant and vigorous in exhortation as the first was rich and full in instruction. The author would show his readers that spiritual wealth is not only to be possessed, but also put to use. The great truths of Christ's superior priesthood and the all-sufficiency of his sacrifice are not just abstractions for the mind but causes of action in daily living.

Briefly as the basis for his rich exhortation the author summarizes the blessings we have in Christ. "Brothers," he calls his readers, identifying himself with them and intensifying his appeal to them. "We," he says to fellow believers, "have confidence to enter the Most Holy Place by the blood of Jesus." Openly and boldly believers can draw near God's

115

presence in heaven. Under the old covenant sinners dared not draw near the symbol of God's presence in the Most Holy Place in the Tabernacle. Only the high priest could and then only once a year and with fear and trembling. Now we can come anytime, without timidity or trembling, to our Father in heaven. "By the blood of Jesus," the author reminds us. There is no other way. His blood in payment for our sins has opened a freeway to heaven which no barricade can ever block and where no toll booth need ever be built.

Look again at that way to heaven. It was "opened," built for us, by Jesus with his death on the cross. It is a "new and living way." The word used for "new" originally meant "freshly slain," a picture quite fitting for Christ our sacrifice. Then it came to mean "recent," again quite fitting for, as Luther said, "It seems but yesterday that Jesus died on the cross." And it is a "living" way. That way is alive and carries those who walk on it to life. That way is Jesus, as he himself said in John 14:6, "I am the WAY and the truth and the LIFE. No one comes to the Father except through me."

Again the author hints at the contrast between the old covenant, to which his readers were tempted to return, and the new, which had brought such great blessings to them. Did they really want to forsake the Son of God, the living way to heaven, for lifeless and ineffective sacrifices? Did they really want to go back to that "curtain" shutting them out from God's presence in the Tabernacle when the "curtain of Christ's body" had brought them free access to the Father's holy throne? With "curtain" the author speaks of Christ's body as being the entrance to heaven. Just as the high priest entered through the ornamental curtain into the Most Holy Place in the Tabernacle so we enter into heaven through Christ's body given for our sins on the cross.

There was even more. Not only do we have complete confidence about the access to heaven, but we have a "great priest" there. He is "over the house of God," which, as already seen in 3:6, refers to God's household of believers. There is no rocking chair in heaven for our great priest, no "now it's all over and it's time for retirement" for him. Instead, he stands before God's face to power us when we struggle with temptation, to plead our cause when we sin, to present us as his brothers when we draw near. Briefly, beautifully the author in these three verses summarizes the matchless blessings we have in Christ before urging us to use them to the utmost.

²²let us draw near to God with a sincere heart in full assurance of faith, having our hearts sprinkled to cleanse us from a guilty conscience and having our bodies washed with pure water. ²³Let us hold unswervingly to the hope we profess, for he who promised is faithful. ²⁴And let us consider how we may spur one another on toward love and good deeds. ²⁵Let us not give up meeting together, as some are in the habit of doing, but let us encourage one another — and all the more as you see the Day approaching.

A series of three stirring exhortations follows. The first deals with the believer and his God. "Let us draw near to God," the author urges, using in the Greek the present tense to indicate such drawing near was never to cease. To draw near our holy God is the believer's blood-bought privilege. How he uses this privilege shows what value he places on it. When men do approach God, only one thing counts, " a sincere heart." God looks beyond persons and positions to the heart.

Let not Christ's complaint to the Pharisees in Matthew 15:8 apply to us: "These people honor me with their lips, but their hearts are far from me." Rather let it be his words in

Matthew 5:8: "Blessed are the pure in heart, for they will see God." Such hearts come "in full assurance of faith." Faith which wavers and wonders, which is easily rattled and roiled up, displays little fulness or certainty. About such faith James 1:6 said, "He who doubts is like a wave of the sea, blown and tossed by the wind."

Why can we have such sincere hearts and full assurance of faith in approaching God? Because we know what blessings we have received in Christ. We have "our hearts sprinkled to cleanse us from a guilty conscience" and "our bodies washed with pure water." Again we note how the author hints at the contrast between the old and new Covenants. The Old Testament high priest in approaching God on the Day of Atonement had to be ceremonially washed and then had to sprinkle animal blood on the Ark of the Covenant (Leviticus 16:4,14). These rituals symbolized the necessity for cleansing before approaching God. No man could approach a holy God with sins' guilt still on his conscience.

Now look at the marvelous cleansing believers have received. It is not symbolic, but actual, covering both the inward "heart" and the outward "body." It is cleansing that needs no repeating. "Sprinkled" and "washed" are Greek verb forms which indicate lasting effects. Both forms are passive, indicating that this sprinkling and washing are done not by, but to us. Also it's a cleansing which involved "blood," as 12:24 shows, and "water."

Clearly Holy Baptism was in the author's mind. The water, applied outwardly to the body and called "pure" because Baptism cleanses, is a symbol of the inward cleansing of the heart by the blood of Jesus. "You are all sons of God through faith in Christ Jesus," Paul puts it in Galatians 3:26,27, "for all of you who were baptized into Christ have been clothed with Christ." God's children, washed clean from all sin by the blood of Jesus, can knock on heaven's door anytime and confidently crawl up on the lap of a waiting, loving Father. Need we be urged to "draw near"? The second exhortation deals with the believer and the world. Cleansed hearts lead to open mouths and speaking lives. The author urges, "Let us hold unswervingly to the hope we profess." Again he uses the present tense to remind us such holding is ever to continue. We might have expected him to write "faith," but he uses "hope" to lift our eyes to the future. From Christ comes not only pardon for sins in the present, but glorious hope for the future. Heaven is our sure home "for he who promised is faithful."

Nothing strengthens our hope for heaven more than the fact of God's faithfulness. How can the Eternal One lie or change his mind? He promised the eternal crown of glory and he will place it on our heads. To such a hope we are to hold "unswervingly," not letting it droop like some banner into the dust, but holding it on high for all to see.

"The hope we profess," the author also said, reminding us that hope is for confession, not concealment. Often confession brings bumps and bruises, sometimes even worse, as the Hebrew Christians had already found out and were again experiencing. But the world's opposition cannot affect our hope. It may hurt our hold on and hinder our confession of the hope, but it cannot harm the hope itself. Those who confess this glorious hope in our modern society have found that opposition is not dead. Yet the world's need for our confession of that hope and God's faithfulness in fulfilling it are still there. "Hold unswervingly" are words of urging for us, too.

The third exhortation deals with the believer and the church. No Christian lives on an island or for himself alone. With his attitudes and actions he has an effect on others.

"Let us consider how we might spur one another on," the author urges, again using the present tense to stress continued action. "Consider" means putting our mind on others, carefully noting their needs. As one body in Christ we need to spur each other on "toward love and good deeds."

The word for love in the Greek is *agape*, the highest kind of love, which loves the undeserving and unlovable, which perceives and then performs. 1 John 4:10 points to the perfect example of such love: "This is love: not that we loved God, but that he loved us and sent his Son as an atoning sacrifice for our sins." Only from such divine love can our love come. We can believe and hope as individuals, but the practice of love always involves others. It also involves "good deeds." When love is present, it is exercised in good deeds toward others, and love must be present for those deeds to be pleasing in God's sight. What a reminder for our age in which the temptation ever lurks, even for the Christian, to consider only "I" and "me" and to be concerned only about "my" and "mine."

How to spur each other on in love and good deeds is stated first negatively, then positively. "Let us not give up meeting together, as some are in the habit of doing" is the negative side. Believers need to gather together to be strengthened and to give strength. Believers go to the gatherings for worship and fellowship not just to gain for themselves, but to give to others. Let the subtle error that believers don't need the church, that they can sit alone at home with their radio or television set on Sunday mornings, be laid to rest by that strong urging. Like blades of grass growing together or charcoal briquettes glowing together, we need each other. Some of those Hebrew Christians had already deserted those gatherings, perhaps out of fear of persecution. How dangerous this could become verses 26-31 will show.

The positive side was, "Let us encourage one another." To encourage does not mean to lecture or criticize. It is the same verb from which is derived the name "Counselor" for the Holy Spirit in John 16:7. Standing alongside and helping each other where needed was far better than giving up meeting with each other. Giving and receiving strength when tempted, urging and being urged when wavering, comforting and being comforted when sorrowing are pluses to be found in gathering around the Word. If the Hebrew Christians needed such urging all the more as they saw the Last Day coming, what about us some 1900 years closer to that Day? "Consider how to spur one another on," the author writes for our benefit, too.

26If we deliberately keep on sinning after we have received the knowledge of the truth, no sacrifice for sins is left, 27but only a fearful expectation of judgment and of raging fire that will consume the enemies of God. 28Anyone who rejected the law of Moses died without mercy on the testimony of two or three witnesses. 29How much more severely do you think a man deserves to be punished who has trampled the Son of God under foot, who has treated as an unholy thing the blood of the covenant that sanctified him, and who has insulted the Spirit of grace? 30For we know him who said, "It is mine to avenge; I will repay," and again, "The Lord will judge his people." 31It is a dreadful thing to fall into the hands of the living God.

Stirring exhortation now turns into stern warning. Giving up meeting together could lead to turning away from faith, so the author warns about the sin against the Holy Ghost. In 6:4-8 he had issued a warning against this same sin so that his readers might pay close attention to what he had to say about the great high priest. Now he repeats the warning to show particularly the dire consequences for those who succumb to this fatal sin.

"If we deliberately keep on sinning after we have received the knowledge of truth," he describes this sin. Here is no sudden sin into which a believer accidentally stumbles, no weak faltering of one just starting to walk in the Spirit. This is willful, deliberate, continued sinning by those who have the knowledge of the saving truth. Verse 27 even labels them "enemies of God."

Did those Jewish Christians realize how serious the sin they were contemplating could be? Certainly persecution's pressure was rubbing their backs sore and they were tempted to desert Christ for the supposed safety of Judaism. But to do so could be fatal. For those who deliberately reject that which they know to be true "no sacrifice for sins is left." The cross on Calvary is final, covering even this sin. But he who has knelt beneath that cross and yet deliberately deserts it has robbed himself of salvation. All that he has left is "a fearful expectation of judgment and of raging fire that will consume the enemies of God."

Note the strong word for such deliberate sinners. They are "enemies of God." There is no middle ground, no mild neutrality, only direct opposition to God and his gracious plan of salvation. For such the future is dreadful, filled only with horrid expectation of God's righteous judgment and the prospect of the seething fires of hell. God's mercy on Calvary's cross satisfied, but did not drown, God's justice. It still stands, as those who reject what his mercy has prepared in Christ will discover to their eternal horror.

An illustration follows to show the seriousness of this sin against the Holy Ghost. The law of Moses, given by God, was highly respected by the Jews. To reject its directives deliberately called for serious punishment. When properly substantiated by two or three witnesses, crimes like idolatry were punished by death (Deuteronomy 17:2-7). For such

122

offenders there was no mercy, only death by stoning. What about punishment then for those rejecting Jesus, who is much greater than Moses, and his new covenant of grace, which is far superior to the old covenant of the law? How much more severely will they be punished?

With three phrases the author details the horribleness and deliberateness of this sin. "He has trampled the Son of God under foot." With deliberate and dirty feet such a sinner stomps all over the highest and best of all beings. He "has treated as an unholy thing the blood of the covenant that sanctified him." With unbelievable insolence such a sinner thumbs his nose at the blood that he had once valued as having cleansed him, now considering it no more than anyone else's blood. "He has insulted the Spirit of grace." From this phrase has come the term the "sin against the Holy Ghost," because such a sinner blasphemes the very agent by whom God's grace is brought to him. We have trouble even describing such a horrible sin, not to mention thinking how anyone could commit it. But it does happen. So the author warns his readers and us.

This warning is no idle threat, as both the author and his readers would know from Old Testament history. In Deuteronomy 32 Moses in his farewell song to Israel recounted what happened when Israel with hardened hearts and against better knowledge had turned away from the Lord. The author quotes the Lord from Deuteronomy 32:35 as saying, "It is mine to avenge: I will repay." Just as Paul in Romans 12:19, so the author does not quote the verse exactly but according to its sense. The certainty of God's vengeance is stressed. Man cannot sin against God with impunity; judgment will follow. What the sinner has earned he will receive.

The second quote from Deuteronomy 32:36 reinforces the thought, "The Lord will judge his people." Israel of old, though God's people, did not escape his righteous judgment. The outward name may be right, but if the heart is hollow, judgment still will come. And what a dreadful thing that judgment is!

To "fall into the hands of the living God," sinking into his caring arms in the day of need, is wonderful indeed. But to fall into those hands when the heart is full of unbelief and sin is nothing short of dreadful. The living God is no "slap-'em-on-the-back" fellow who with a wink of the eye says, "That's okay." He means it with eternal seriousness when he says in Mark 16:16, "Whoever does not believe will be condemned." Let the 20th century preacher sound forth the siren of this warning as clearly as did the first century author of the letter to the Hebrews. And let sinners of every century listen carefully!

32Remember those earlier days after you had received the light, when you stood your ground in a great contest in the face of suffering. 33Sometimes you were publicly exposed to insult and persecution; at other times you stood side by side with those who were so treated. 34You sympathized with those in prison and joyfully accepted the confiscation of your property, because you knew that you yourselves had better and lasting possessions.

As a wise and loving pastor the author dwells on the negative no longer than he has to. Quickly he moves from warning to encouragement by taking his readers back to their "earlier days" in the faith. "Keep remembering those earlier days after you had received the light," he urges. When the Holy Spirit had first lit up their hearts with faith, friends had forsaken and foes had hounded them. Those earlier days had not been easy, but a "great contest in the face of suffering." "Contest" is a Greek word from which our word "athletics" comes and points to the strenuousness involved.

Their suffering had been intense, but they had "stood their ground." In the first flush of faith, like the early Christians in Jerusalem in Acts 5:41, they had endured, rejoicing that "they had been counted worthy of suffering disgrace for the Name."

Details of the "great contest" follow. Sometimes the believers "were publicly exposed to insult and persecution." "Publicly exposed," a word used only here in the New Testament, is the same one from which our word "theater" comes. In some way those Hebrew Christians had been publicly exposed and disgraced by the enemies of the faith. Insults and persecutions always hurt and even more so when publicly inflicted.

Other times the believers got into trouble because they stood "side by side" with those who were being persecuted. Though silence could have spelled safety for them, they instead bravely "sympathized with those in prison." In those days prisoners often had to depend on relatives and friends for daily provisions, one reason why Christ in Matthew 25:36 says, "I was in prison and you came to visit me." To visit Christians in prison meant to be identified with them and run the risk of sharing their fate. Yet this risk those sympathetic Christians had bravely taken. When identified as Christians, they had also suffered personally as their homes were broken into and plundered.

Did the readers remember those earlier days? Then they also had to remember that only good had come out of them. Persecution had forged bonds of fellowship so that they stood side by side with fellow believers. Persecution had developed resiliency of faith so that they could "joyfully" accept the loss of property. Persecution had sharpened their priorities so that heaven's "better and lasting possessions" were most highly prized.

Others may tolerate trouble, but only believers can take it joyfully. They have heard the Savior promise in Matthew 5:11,12, "Blessed are you when people insult you, persecute you, and falsely say all kinds of evil against you because of me. Rejoice and be glad, because great is your reward in heaven." Could it be that the absence of persecution and the presence of prosperity have removed some of the value from Christ's treasures and some of the urgency from the church's task for modern Christians? Think about it!

35So do not throw away your confidence; it will be richly rewarded. 36You need to persevere so that when you have done the will of God, you will receive what he has promised. 37For in just a very little while, "He who is coming will come and will not delay. 38But my righteous one will live by faith. And if he shrinks back, I will not be pleased with him." 39But we are not of those who shrink back and are destroyed, but of those who believe and are saved.

The remembrance of God's help in earlier days sets the stage for the author's exhortation, "So do not throw away your confidence." Under the strain of present persecution they were not recklessly to reject what they had recognized earlier as being so valuable. Regardless what came, they were to cling to their confidence in Christ. "It will be richly rewarded," the author promises them. The heaven which a faithful God has promised is for real and rich beyond measure.

This was no time to lose confidence and drop out like drained athletes or battle-weary soldiers. Instead they needed to "persevere," a rich word meaning to bear up patiently under heavy loads. What awaited them was just too valuable to lose. Those who do the will of God will receive full salvation in heaven. Lest we think that doing the will of God involves merit on our part and a partial earning of heaven by our own works, we quote Jesus from John 6:40, "For my Father's will is that everyone who looks to the Son and believes in him shall have eternal life, and I will raise him up at the last day." The words of Revelation 2:10, "Be faithful, even to the point of death, and I will give you the crown of life," are a good commentary on this verse.

We have already seen how the author lived in the Scriptures, so we are not surprised when we find him reinforcing his exhortation with an Old Testament quotation. This time he turns to Habakkuk 2:3,4. The discerning reader will note that the author quotes freely, but without altering the meaning. The Holy Spirit uses the pen of the author of the letter to the Hebrews to convey the fuller meaning of Habakkuk's words. They are God's words, given by him to Habakkuk and now interpreted by him through the author of Hebrews.

"He who is coming" refers to Christ, who came to Bethlehem and will come again on the Last Day. "He will come," the author reminds the readers positively and then reinforces it negatively, "He will not delay." The persecution coming on those Christians might be drastic and Christ's return might seem distant, but it was "just a very little while" when compared to eternity. Through the ages God's beleaguered people have found encouragement in the message of the coming Christ. While we wait through this little while, faithfulness is so important.

Those who have been made "righteous" through faith in Christ "will live by faith." They live in an atmosphere of trust, leaning on God's promises, learning to see the invisible, looking ahead to eternity. The opposite is to shrink back as a cowardly turncoat and to experience the eternal woe involved when the Lord says, "I will not be pleased with him."

Which would it be for those hesitating Hebrew Christians? The author has warned them strongly, but he is not ready to give up on them. Identifying himself with them, he confidently states, "We are not of those who shrink back and are destroyed, but of those who believe and are saved."

Are any tired Christians reading these words? Any weary warriors who have found that the world still knows how to persecute souls who dare to speak out for Christ? Any licking invisible wounds received for standing against what is wrong and for what is right? Any perhaps for the sake of ease tempted to let the Savior's banner dip and the scriptural confession drag? Then it's time to reread these verses of Hebrews.

Martin Luther, expounding on this section of Hebrews to his students in that extremely difficult year of 1517 when he nailed up the 95 Theses, remarked, "He who relies on Christ through faith is carried on the shoulders of Christ." The faithful are carried on the shoulders of a loving Savior. He bears them safely to the very mansions of heaven. To him we draw near, not back. And that is done only through his word!

Let Us Remember the Heroes of Faith

11 Now faith is being sure of what we hope for and certain of what we do not see. [2] This is what the ancients were commended for.

Having ended the previous section by referring to the necessity of faith, it was only natural that the author pick up on that thought. What follows is the grandest chapter in the Bible on faith. The author does not pretend to say all there is to say about faith. He gives us not so much a definition as a description of faith. This he does in a most concrete way by pointing to examples of faith in the Old Testament. Before us he sets the heroes of faith, men and women who had faith's 20/20 vision and as a result trusted God's promises of what they could not see with their natural eyes and endured persecution which they could not have borne with their own strength. A walk through this gallery of saints, this "hall of faith," will do the reader of any century much good.

What does the author mean with the word "faith"? It is not some hunch-following, some blind leaping into the dark. Nor is it some hoping for the best, blithely disregarding facts and assuming all will be well. "Faith is being sure of what we hope for," the author states. "Being sure" means having solid confidence. Faith brings the future into the present because it makes things hoped for as real as if we already had them. Christ's second coming in glory and our full enjoyment of eternal salvation are not only hoped for, but real to the believer. Faith is being "certain of what we do not see," the author continues. "Being sure" and "being certain" are synonymns, both describing faith's solid confidence. "What we hope for" points more to the future while "what we do not see" is much wider, covering all the divine realities from the first day of creation to the last day of the universe.

Though we have not seen the creation or the crucifixion, though we were not present to witness the flood waters rising above the mountain peaks or the Savior rising triumphantly from the Easter tomb, though we have not heard his actual voice pardoning our sins and promising his return, yet we believe. For the believer faith is a sixth sense making the invisible seen and certain.

The author could have said much more about faith. He might have pointed to faith's origin, how it is worked by the Spirit through the gospel in word and sacrament. He might have more fully pointed out faith's basis, how it rests on God's eternal Word which 1 Peter 1:25 says "stands forever." But instead, he is content with describing faith's

129

nature. Pointing to the examples of the Old Testament heroes of faith, he would show his readers that faith trusts God absolutely, that faith is convinced what God says is true and what he promises will come to pass. Those "ancients" had this confident trust in both the future and the unseen and were commended by God because of it. He gave them an *A* by recording their faith on the pages of the Old Testament. For Hebrew Christians beginning to doubt God's promises and tempted to walk by sight instead of faith, this record was important. For us, too!

³By faith we understand that the universe was formed at God's command, so that what is seen was not made out of what was visible.

Before taking us on the tour down the "hall of faith," the author turns back to Scripture's first page. The very first line of the Bible presupposes and demands faith such as the author has just described. No one else was there when "the universe was formed," only the eternal God, and he has recorded what took place. It was "at his command" that heaven and earth and all that fills them through the ages came into being. "Let there be," he said as Genesis 1 records, "and it was so."

Only by faith can we accept that everything we see around us was not made out of things visible to us. We place our trust not on what others who were not there have to say or theorize, but on what he who was there has been pleased to tell us. Could the author have found a better example for faith as he has described it?

⁴By faith Abel offered God a better sacrifice than Cain did. By faith he was commended as a righteous man, when God spoke well of his offerings. And by faith he still speaks, even though he is dead. ⁵By faith Enoch was taken from this life, so that he did not

experience death; he could not be found, because God had taken him away. For before he was taken, he was commended as one who pleased God. ⁶And without faith it is impossible to please God, because anyone who comes to him must believe that he exists and that he rewards those who earnestly seek him. ⁷By faith Noah, when warned about things not yet seen, in holy fear built an ark to save his family. By his faith he condemned the world and became an heir of the righteousness that comes by faith.

The first portrait on the wall of the "hall of faith" is Abel's. Genesis 4:1-15 records the account of his faith. Abel offered "a better sacrifice than Cain did," not because of what he brought, but because of why he brought it. Then, as now, God looked beyond the offering to the giver and the heart from which it came. This fact Genesis 4:4 records, "The Lord looked with favor on Abel and his offering," pointing first to the giver and then to the gift. But then, just as now, when the Lord testifies about faith, he does so by pointing to the gifts faith brings. In the Last Judgment that will still be the case, as Jesus reminds us in Matthew 25:34-40.

God gave approval to Abel as "a righteous man," one who could stand just and holy in his divine presence, not because of what Abel did, but because of what he was by faith. Abel trusted the unseen promises of God about the coming Savior, and his actions showed it. God granted his approval by recording Abel's faith on the pages of Holy Scripture so that this first man who ever died might still speak to us today. "Faith's way may be rugged," Abel would remind us, "but God's grace is sufficient and his smile of approval sweet."

Next on the wall hangs the portrait of Enoch. His biography in Genesis 5:21-24 occupies only a few lines, but how much those lines tell us! He "was one who pleased God," the author says, using the Septuagint's translation of the Hebrew which in Genesis 5:24 says, "Enoch walked with God."

"By faith" Enoch did this. Enoch trusted and walked in God's promises. God's approval was shown in Enoch's being taken to heaven both body and soul without experiencing death. Just as to Elijah of later date, this marvelous and miraculous translation was granted him by a gracious God. What a preview of the Last Day when as Paul records in 1 Corinthians 15:51,52, "We will not all sleep, but we will all be changed — in a flash, in the twinkling of an eye, at the last trumpet."

Even though the Old Testament record did not use the word "faith" of Enoch, the author reminds us, that's what it was. "Without faith," he says, "it is impossible to please God." "Impossible," he said, emphasizing faith's necessity. Those who would come to God in worshipful trust must be convinced that he exists and that he graciously rewards those who genuinely seek his promises. Such faith Enoch had by the grace of God, and to such faith God gave approval in a most striking way. "Believing is seeing," Enoch might tell us, from the vantage points of both earth and heaven.

Noah's portrait is next, as we would expect. Talk about being convinced of "things not seen"! Noah lived on dry land, perhaps had never seen the sea, most certainly had never seen a flood rising above the highest mountain top, yet when "warned," when divinely instructed by God, he started building the ark. "Holy fear" galvanized him into action. Unbelieving fear terrorizes and paralyzes; godly fear stands in awe of God and goes into action at his command.

So by faith Noah built that battleship of an ark on dry land. For 120 years this "preacher of righteousness," as 2 Peter 2:5 describes him, built and by his very actions, if not also by his words, "condemned the world." Almost alone in a totally corrupt world, he trusted God and his promises and became the possessor of the righteousness that comes only by faith. Noah was saved, not only from the waters of the flood, but also from the fires of hell, through faith in God's promises.

Do we feel that we are all alone in the world, that perhaps we are wrong and all the others right? "Never mind," Noah might answer, "in my day eight were right and all the others perished."

[8]By faith Abraham, when called to go to a place he would later receive as his inheritance, obeyed and went, even though he did not know where he was going. [9]By faith he made his home in the promised land like a stranger in a foreign country; he lived in tents, as did Isaac and Jacob, who were heirs with him of the same promise. [10]For he was looking forward to the city with foundations, whose architect and builder is God.

Before Abraham's portrait the author would have his readers pause a bit longer. It was only natural that he would assign the central spot in the "hall of faith" to the Father of the Faithful. Consistently Abraham trusted God, taking him at his word and following his direction even when there was nothing to see and even more so when what could be seen pointed only to the seemingly impossible. Not knowing the direction, trusting God's directive, he left his homeland in Mesopotamia. With no map in hand, but with God's call in his heart, Abraham went out into the unknown. Faith is that way! It is content to go forward blindfolded because it trusts God's leading.

That unknown land was to be his inheritance, but all he ever owned of Canaan was a burial plot purchased when his beloved Sarah died (Genesis 23). God "gave him no inheritance there, not even a foot of ground," Stephen recounted in Acts 7:5, marveling at the patriarch's faith. Like some foreigner he moved his tent from place to place in the land that had been promised to him; nor was it any different for his son Isaac and his grandson Jacob. They died not having seen, but having trusted God's promise.

How could Abraham do it? The author has one answer, "By faith." By faith Abraham saw the invisible. In fact, it is amazing just how far Abraham's faith saw. He even looked beyond the earthly Canaan to the eternal city in heaven. In this city, belonging wholly to God because he was its architect and actual builder, Abraham saw his real home. This was the city "with foundations." Tents have only pegs which are pulled up and moved. Earthly cities have walls which stand longer and yet crumble. But this city stands forever. "The heavenly Jerusalem, the city of the living God," the author describes it in 12:22 so that we cannot misunderstand. To this heavenly home Abraham "was looking forward," ever living and finally dying in expectation of it. How shortsighted we are at times! How foolish at times when we turn the binoculars around and focus in on earth's sand rather than heaven's shores.

[11]By faith Abraham, even though he was past age — and Sarah herself was barren — was enabled to become a father because he considered him faithful who had made the promise. [12]And so from this one man, and he as good as dead, came descendants as numerous as the stars in the sky and as countless as the sand on the seashore.

"By faith" also Abraham "was enabled to become a father." He was 99 years old, past the age of begetting a child, when Isaac's coming birth was announced to him. Sarah also was barren, and yet the two conceived a child by God's miraculous working. From such a small beginning — "this one man" — and from such a miraculous beginning — "he as good as dead" — came descendants as countless as the proverbial stars in the sky and sand on the seashore.

Physically all Israel counts its beginning from Abraham; spiritually all believers in his greatest descendant, Christ, call him father. So rich was the harvest that came from him, and it came by faith! Abraham "considered him faithful who had made the promise." Abraham trusted a God who could never be unfaithful and a promise which therefore could not remain unfulfilled. When it comes to God and his promises, the word "impossible" does not belong in a Christian's vocabulary.

[13]All these people were still living by faith when they died. They did not receive the things promised; they only saw them and welcomed them from a distance. And they admitted that they were aliens and strangers on earth. [14]People who say such things show that they are looking for a country of their own. [15]If they had been thinking of the country they had left, they would have had opportunity to return. [16]Instead, they were longing for a better country — a heavenly one. Therefore God is not ashamed to be called their God, for he has prepared a city for them.

The author has more to say about Abraham's faith. Before he does, though, he pauses to emphasize some common qualities found in Abraham's faith as well as in the faith of the other patriarchs. All these died without receiving the things promised. Abraham and Isaac, Jacob and Joseph never saw God's promises fulfilled. Though Abraham lived to see Isaac's birth, he never saw the great nation which was to come from him. Though Jacob and Joseph saw this nation begin to grow, they never saw the Messiah who was to come from it. Yet they believed! Like Moses on Mt. Nebo, viewing the promised land from a distance (Deuteronomy 32:52), they saw God's promises from afar and believed them. Faith's telescope brought God's promises into view so that the patriarchs are pictured as waiting in joyful anticipation of them.

They admitted "that they were aliens and strangers on earth." This was Abraham's confession in Genesis 23:4 when buying the burial plot for Sarah, but it was characteristic of all the heroes of faith. They were "aliens," people of foreign descent and culture living in another land. They were "strangers," people residing temporarily someplace other than in their real home. More than Canaan was meant with this confession. The author rightly concludes, "People who say such things show they are looking for a country of their own." "Country" means "fatherland," the home from which you come and for which you long. Faith implants in the believer a homing instinct that will not allow him to root or rest here on earth.

It was not of Mesopotamia the patriarchs were thinking when they looked for their homeland. If Abraham had wanted to return there, it would have been easy. All he had to do was pack his bags, pull up his tent stakes, and go. Jacob, when having served his uncle Laban twenty years in that very land, still wasn't satisfied. In Genesis 30:25 he begged his uncle, "Send me on my way so I can go back to my own homeland," namely Canaan.

Not Mesopotamia, not Canaan was on their minds and in their hearts, but "a better country — a heavenly one." Toward the heavenly Canaan and the new Jerusalem, prepared for them by God, they stretched forth faith's hand in earnest longing all their days. No wonder God was not ashamed to be called their God.

To have God give us his name by bringing us to faith and into his family is great indeed. To have him take our name because of our God-given faith makes us catch our breath in wonder at his grace. In Exodus 3:6 he called himself, "the God of Abraham, the God of Isaac and the God of Jacob," and Jesus in Matthew 22:32 says the same. God grant that our names be added to the list!

Can you read this section without being both rebuked and encouraged? "I'm but a stranger here, Heav'n is my home," we love to sing (TLH 660), but in life's reality it's often so different. Eyes that should be raised heavenward are riveted on earth. Feet that should be tramping toward Canaan's shores are mired in earth's swamps. Hands that should be reaching for eternal treasures are wrapped around gaudy marbles. Backs that should be straining in kingdom effort are bent over in valueless pursuit.

What a rebuke those portraits of faith speak to us. But also what encouragement. "Press on," those portraits tell us, "it's worth it. The God you trust is absolutely reliable. He means what he says and does what he promises. He said that heaven is your home and there you shall surely stand, with us, at his right hand."

17By faith Abraham, when God tested him, offered Isaac as a sacrifice. He who had received the promises was about to sacrifice his one and only son, 18even though God had said to him, "It is through Isaac that your offspring will be reckoned." 19Abraham reasoned that God could raise the dead, and figuratively speaking, he did receive Isaac back from death.

Once more the author would have us look at Abraham's portrait. In Genesis 22 we find Abraham's faith at its height. What God asked of him must have seemed not only incredible, but completely contrary to all that God had promised. Abraham was to take his one and only son by Sarah, the son born of his old age and so dear to him and sacrifice him to God. Even more, that son was the one through whom God

137

Abraham's Offering of Isaac

had promised in Genesis 21:12 that Abraham's offspring would be reckoned. Romans 9:6-9 shows the wider significance of this promise. From Isaac would come not only physical Israel, but spiritual Israel, composed of all true believers in Christ, Abraham's greatest seed. To sacrifice Isaac seemed to mean canceling the fulfillment of that glorious promise.

But God's test was met by Abraham's obedient faith. About the Gethsemane Abraham went through that night after receiving God's command the Bible says nothing. It does, however, record the obedience of his faith. Early the next morning Abraham moved forward in compliance with God's command. The author of Hebrews even says that Abraham "offered Isaac as a sacrifice." In Abraham's mind the deed was as good as done, so obedient was his faith to God's command.

When tested, Abraham's faith obeyed. When tested, his faith also trusted God's promises. "Abraham reasoned that God could raise the dead." Abraham showed this faith when at the foot of Mt. Moriah in Genesis 22:5 he told his servants, "Stay here . . . while I and the boy go over there. We will worship and then WE will come back to you." With the logic of faith Abraham reasoned that God who had given him Isaac when he was as good as dead could give him back Isaac from the dead. And figuratively speaking, that's what happened. Abraham had wholeheartedly given Isaac over to God only to receive him back as from the dead.

Lord, give us such a faith as this, a faith which not only can move mountains, but also defy death, a faith which because of the death and resurrection of Abraham's greater Seed, the Christ, can now shout with Paul in 1 Corinthians 15:55,57, " 'Where, O death, is your victory? Where, O death, is your sting?'... Thanks be to God! He gives us the victory through our Lord Jesus Christ."

²⁰By faith Isaac blessed Jacob and Esau in regard to their future. ²¹By faith Jacob, when he was dying, blessed each of Joseph's sons, and worshiped as he leaned on the top of his staff. ²²By faith Joseph, when his end was near, spoke about the exodus of the Israelites from Egypt and gave instructions about his bones.

The next three patriarchs whose portraits are presented illustrate faith's farsightedness. Though the author might have selected a number of scenes from their lives, he chooses only one apiece, each from their closing days. These three scenes present Isaac, Jacob and Joseph's faith as looking beyond their death. They were confident that God would fulfill his promises even though they did not live to see them. Isaac, blind and aged, could not see which son was kneeling before him, but with the eyes of faith he could see what the future held for each of them. Genesis 27:1 — 28:5 records how he gave Jacob the promise of the Savior from his seed and Esau promises of an earthly nature.

Jacob in his earlier days had leaned too heavily on his own resources and skill, but on his deathbed he leaned on his staff in worshipful trust in God's faithfulness. Only his blessing of Joseph's two sons, whom Jacob had adopted as his own, is mentioned here while the whole account can be read in Genesis 47:28 — 49:33. The dying patriarch in speaking blessings far off in the future viewed them as already fulfilled.

Joseph, though he could have had his body impressively preserved in some Egyptian pyramid, looked ahead with eyes of faith through the mist of 400 years to Canaan. Genesis 50:22-26 records how this mighty man of Egypt bound his family by oath to bury him in Canaan, a land in which he had spent only the first seventeen years of his life. His words about the exodus from Egypt and his instructions about his bones revealed his faith in God's promises. His bones were to be buried in the land where the promise of salvation would be fulfilled. What an example of a faith that was "sure of what we hope for and certain of what we do not see." What encouragement for us whose faith so often trusts so little and whose eyes so seldom see very far.

[23]By faith Moses' parents hid him for three months after he was born, because they saw he was no ordinary child, and they were not afraid of the king's edict. [24]By faith Moses, when he had grown up, refused to be known as the son of Pharaoh's daughter. [25]He chose to be mistreated along with the people of God rather than to enjoy the pleasures of sin for a short time. [26]He regarded disgrace for the sake of Christ as of greater value than the treasures of Egypt, because he was looking ahead to his reward. [27]By faith he left Egypt, not fearing the king's anger; he persevered because he saw him who is invisible. [28]By faith he kept the Passover and the sprinkling of blood, so that the destroyer of the firstborn would not touch the firstborn of Israel.

From Genesis and the patriarchs it is just a step down the "hall of faith" to Exodus and Moses. Before Moses' portrait the author pauses for a while giving us several examples of his faith. Was the author trying to say something to readers tempted to desert Christianity and Christ for Judaism and Moses? Let them look closely at Moses and find in him one of the greatest examples of faith in Christ.

The author takes us back to Exodus 1-2 where the account begins with Moses' God-fearing parents. In Exodus 1:22 the great Pharaoh of Egypt had given the order, "Every boy that is born you must throw into the river, but let every girl live." Moses' parents weren't afraid of the royal edict. Instead, they hid their baby boy for three months after his birth.

Joy at their baby's birth must have been dampened by concern when they saw it was a boy. Anxiety must have shadowed every day of those three months as they struggled to keep quiet and secret a growing baby boy. But they did it — "by faith." "They saw that he was no ordinary child," or as Exodus 2:2 says, "he was a fine child."

Did the parents, knowing God's promise of the exodus and seeing the exceptional quality of their child, hope he would be the one to lead God's people out? We aren't told, but this much we do know. By faith they hid that baby, trusting that somehow God would protect him. Here was faith that trusted God for the unseen and the hoped for.

From the baby of three months the author takes us to the grown man. Stephen in Acts 7:21,22 reminds us of the privileges Moses had: "Pharaoh's daughter took him and brought him up as her own son. Moses was educated in all the wisdom of the Egyptians and was powerful in speech and action." Now as a grown man, perhaps at age 40 (Acts 7:23), Moses made a decision. "He refused," it says, he said *no* to the elite position and exalted privileges he had as the son of Pharaoh's daughter. "By faith" he did this, knowing what his decision would cost him. Deliberately he shook off the position of royal blood and chose identification with the people of God.

With this decision he showed faith in the future destiny of those who now looked only like slaves. From his decision came mistreatment; what the people of God were going through fell on him. It could be no other way for this man of faith. For Moses to remain in Pharaoh's court even after knowing that God had called him to rescue Israel (Acts 7:25) would have been sin. Sin's pleasures are only for a short time when compared to what God has in store for his people. Were the Hebrew readers listening and thinking?

Moses faced a situation much like theirs and by faith chose Christ.

The author has more to say about Moses' choice. Egypt's treasures were tremendous as historians and archaeologists have well documented. Moses, however, knew a greater treasure, "disgrace for the sake of Christ." Disgrace suffered for Christ's sake Moses valued as priceless honor. Yes, Moses knew about Christ. He himself said so in Deuteronomy 18:15 when he urged Israel to look for and listen to that greater Prophet who was coming. Jesus also said so when he told the Pharisees in John 5:46, "Moses wrote about me." With the eye of faith Moses saw the coming Christ and identified with him by joining his people.

What did it matter if suffering resulted? Moses "was looking ahead to his reward." Faith's eye sees not only the present, but especially the future. Faith's wisdom calculates not only the beginning, but especially the ending. By faith Moses looked for the same heavenly city as Abraham (11:10) and the other patriarchs (11:16). Their example reminds us of Paul's words in 2 Corinthians 4:18, "So we fix our eyes not on what is seen, but on what is unseen. For what is seen is temporary, but what is unseen is eternal." Doesn't their example urge us to recheck our calculations?

Forty years earlier Moses had fled in fear from the face of this mighty Pharaoh to Midian (Exodus 2:15). Now he leads Israel out, never to return. Pharaoh's anger would flare again and make him hotly pursue the exiting Israelites, but Moses was not afraid. He stood firm "because he saw him who is invisible." Where his Lord led he would go and what strength he needed his Lord would provide. How could Moses see and trust him who is invisible? With the eyes of faith, the author reminds us. So does Peter in 1 Peter 1:8, "Though you have not seen him, you love him; and even

The Waters Are Divided

The Egyptians Are Destroyed

though you do not see him now, you believe in him and are filled with inexpressible and glorious joy." How's our vision?

Plague after plague, nine in all, had come, but Pharaoh had not let Israel go. Now came the announcement of the tenth plague. The firstborn in every home in Egypt would die except where the blood of the lamb had been sprinkled on the lintels and the doorposts. Also the people were to eat the Passover meal on the ready, waiting for the signal to march. And Moses believed what he had not seen!

The destroying angel came, but passed over the homes sprinkled with blood. Israel marched out of Egypt, and Moses, as God had commanded, set the Passover as an annual reminder of God's deliverance. All this he did by faith! He who might have gained for himself a line or two in Egyptian history is instead immortalized on the pages of God's Holy Word and privileged to stand on the Mount of Transfiguration with the Savior for whose coming he had waited (Matthew 17:3).

29By faith the people passed through the Red Sea as on dry land; but when the Egyptians tried to do so, they were drowned. 30By faith the walls of Jericho fell, after the people had marched around them for seven days. 31By faith the prostitute Rahab, because she welcomed the spies, was not killed with those who were disobedient.

The people shared Moses' faith, at least at first. Later their faith would turn into the bitter grumbling of unbelief in the wilderness, but at the Red Sea it still shone forth. Exodus 14 records how all Israel walked on dry land between those towering water walls to safety on the opposite shore. That was more than courage. Pharaoh and Egypt's crack troops had courage, too, but the Red Sea's cascading waters drank them down to the last man. Israel passed safely through by trusting God's promise. The Red Sea was no barrier to their faith, neither were the walls of Jericho's frowning fortress. Those walls were built to withstand the assaults of mighty armies, but not the tramp and the trump and the triumphant shout of faith. Incredibly the walls fell on that seventh day as faith became sight.

Within Jericho's walls was one who also saw by faith, Rahab the prostitute. By God's amazing grace this woman of tarnished profession and Gentile background had come to know and trust the God of Israel. Joshua 2 records her faith and her actions in hiding Israel's spies who had come in advance into Jericho. By faith she risked her life and ended up saving it. While all the other inhabitants, described as "disobedient" because that's what unbelief is, were killed, Rahab and her family were spared in Jericho's fall. And by God's grace her portrait hangs in the "hall of faith."

32And what more shall I say? I do not have time to tell about Gideon, Barak, Samson, Jephthah, David, Samuel and the prophets, 33who through faith conquered kingdoms, administered justice, and gained what was promised; who shut the mouths of lions, 34quenched the fury of the flames, and escaped the edge of the sword; whose weakness was turned into strength; and who became powerful in battle and routed the foreign armies. 35Women received back their dead, raised to life again. Others were tortured and refused to be released, so that they might gain a better resurrection. 36Some faced jeers and flogging, while still others were chained and put in prison. 37They were stoned, they were sawed in two; they were put to death by the sword. They went about in sheepskins and goatskins, destitute, persecuted and mistreated — 38the world was not worthy of them. They wandered in deserts and mountains, and in caves and holes in the ground.

The author is running out of time, not examples. How could he mention all the heroes of faith from Israel's history? So he generalizes, listing six notable names, not in chronological order, but as the Spirit brings them to mind, and also listing some achievements and sufferings of the heroes of faith.

Of the six names five are from the dark period of the Judges. By faith Gideon, as Judges 6-8 records, defeated Midian's mighty army with a handful of 300 men. By faith Barak, as recorded in Judges 4-5, along with Deborah was God's man of the hour to defeat the Canaanites. By faith Samson in Judges 13-16 defeated the Philistines a number of times. By faith Jephthah faced the Ammonites and defeated them with God's power as related in Judges 11-12.

From judges the author proceeds to kings and mentions an illustrious one. All would know of David's deeds both against Goliath and for Israel. Of the prophets he mentions only one, Samuel, who had been a beacon of faith in a darkening chapter of Israel's history.

See how wisely the author picks his examples. Were the Hebrew readers facing difficult circumstances? Here were six men who stood against hopeless odds and came out on top. Faith for them was not just talk, but trust in action.

Like a drum roll the author beats out their daring accomplishments of faith. They grappled with kingdoms and brought them into the dust. Was the author thinking of David's victories recorded in 2 Samuel 8? "They administered justice" in the policies they followed as leaders. 2 Samuel 8:15 says of David, "He reigned over all Israel, doing what was just and right for all his people." Gideon, Barak, David are just a few of those who launched forth against the enemy on the basis of God's promises and found those promises to be true.

Daniel faced the lions in their den and found their mouths locked (Daniel 6:21-23). Shadrach, Meshach and Abednego were thrown into the seven-fold fire of Nebuchadnezzar's furnace and emerged without a whiff of smoke on them (Daniel 3:27). Elijah and others moved among drawn swords which could not reach them (1 Kings 19:1-3). Samson's weakness became strength when the blinded but penitent warrior collapsed Dagon's temple on the heads of thousands of Philistines (Judges 16:30). David, when he toppled mighty Goliath (1 Samuel 17:50), and Israel, when they took on greatly superior enemy forces, are examples of those "who became powerful in battle and routed foreign armies."

Has God's hand been shortened and his power reduced? Are his promises less true today, and is his presence less near? Then let us take a fresh grip on the sword of the spirit and do brave battle against the unholy triple alliance of the devil, the world and our flesh. Only death brings an end to such warfare and only God can grant victory. Faith knows and dares.

From examples of faith's daring the author turns to examples of faith's enduring. 1 Kings 17:17-24 records how the widow of Zarephath received her son back from the dead by Elijah's prayer and the Lord's power. So did the Shunamite in 2 Kings 4:18-37 from the hands of Elisha. Both mothers tasted the bitter grief of loss, but had it turned into joy by the resurrection. Others, when tortured for their faith, died looking for a better resurrection. "Tortured" refers to a gruesome instrument of torture, wheel shaped, on which the victims would be stretched taut and then beaten till they broke or breathed their last. A simple denial of Christ would have kept them away or released them from that horrid wheel, but it would also have lost them eternity. These martyrs prized the resurrection to come as far greater in value than earthly life.

God's prophets knew all about vicious and cruel jeering. 2 Chronicles 36:16 tells us, "They mocked God's messengers, despised his words and scoffed at his prophets until the wrath of the Lord was aroused against his people and there was no remedy." Jeremiah 20:2 records how that great prophet felt flogging's sting. Joseph knew about chains and prisons (Genesis 39:20) and so did Micaiah (1 Kings 22:27).

The list of indignities suffered for Christ continues. Some, like the prophet Zechariah, met death by stoning at the hands of their own countrymen (2 Chronicles 24:20,21). Others, such as tradition claims for Isaiah, were gruesomely "sawed in two." 1 Kings 19:10 states that Israel "put God's prophets to death with the sword." Years later, in his parable of the vineyard in Matthew 21:35,36, Jesus sadly reminded Israel, "The tenants seized his (God's) servants; they beat one, killed another, and stoned a third. Then he sent other servants to them, more than the first time, and the tenants treated them the same way." Those who escaped barely eked out an existence. Scantily dressed in sheepskins and goatskins, lacking even many of the essentials of life, constantly mistreated and persecuted by those they had come to serve, they wandered about the land. Like wild animals always on the move, they roamed through desert and mountain, hiding and sleeping in dank caves and dark holes in the ground.

No matter! Don't feel sorry for them. They valued earthly comfort little compared to the eternal Christ. Earth's safety was secondary when placed alongside eternal salvation. Earth's home shrank in importance when compared to heaven's mansions. They would not deny their Lord! And those whom the world valued little God calls worth far more than the whole world. See how he prizes faith that endures in the face of suffering. See how he gives strength to endure.

And we so often hesitate to live by faith lest the world throw its dirty digs at us and paste some derisive label on us.

³⁹These were all commended for their faith, yet none of them received what had been promised. ⁴⁰God had planned something better for us so that only together with us would they be made perfect.

In our tour through the "hall of faith" the author, by giving name and example, has drawn attention to many. Their inclusion on the pages of the Old Testament shows God's approval of their faith. Their striking examples stand for us, showing how God, when he works faith, moves ordinary people to do extraordinary things. Yet one thing was missing for all of these heroes of faith mentioned. They had received and seen fulfilled many promises from God, but Christ's coming to the cross and his coming on the Last Day had not occurred during their lifetime. Only from a distance with faith's telescope did they see these events.

This delay was for us! God's goal in keeping those Old Testament heroes of faith waiting for the final fulfillment of his promises was that we might join their ranks. God still delays so that "many will come from the east and the west, and will take their places at the feast with Abraham, Isaac and Jacob in the kingdom of heaven," as Jesus pointed out in Matthew 8:11. With the eye of faith we join the hymn-writer in anticipating the scene when "Ten thousand times ten thousand, in sparkling raiment bright, the armies of the ransomed saints, throng up the steeps of light. 'Tis finished, all is finished, their fight with death and sin; fling open wide the golden gates and let the victors in."

Note, though, the author writes, "God had planned something better for us." Those Old Testament heroes of faith are no second-class citizens in heaven. Christ's cross reaches with its redemption both backward to them and forward to us. But those heroes of faith operated on so much less than we do. They lived in the shadow and yet dared and died for Christ. They had so little and yet did so much.

Do we catch the challenge the author is placing before his New Testament readers? The full triumph of the cross is ours. The full truths of God's promises are in our hands. Now what will we do and dare for him? Will our portraits, by the grace of God, be added on the walls of the "hall of faith"? Will a gracious God count us among those who have done the only great things this world has ever really known?

> Lord, give us such a faith as this;
> And then, whate'er may come,
> We'll taste e'en now the hallowed bliss
> Of an eternal home.

Let Us Grow in Faith Through God's Discipline

12 Therefore, since we are surrounded by such a great cloud of witnesses, let us throw off everything that hinders and the sin that so easily entangles, and let us run with perseverance the race marked out for us. ²Let us fix our eyes on Jesus, the author and perfecter of our faith, who for the joy set before him endured the cross, scorning its shame, and sat down at the right hand of the throne of God. ³Consider him who endured such opposition from sinful men, so that you will not grow weary and lose heart.

Skillfully the author in the last chapter has sketched the importance of persistent faith. Like some massive cloud those Old Testament heroes of faith surround the readers, giving vivid example of the endurance and eventual triumph of faith. "Don't give up!" those heroes would shout from the pages of Holy Scripture, "Keep on running! You're on the right track!"

It's a familiar picture the author employs now for his exhortation about perseverance in faith. "The race," he calls it, using the Greek word from which our word "agony" comes. He's talking about a contest involving exertion and struggle. He's also talking about a constant contest, for in the Greek he wrote, "Let us keep on running." And he's talking about an extremely difficult contest, one which requires perseverance. Perseverance means holding out under stress, not slowing down or stopping for any reason. The race of faith is not some hundred-meter dash, but a life-long marathon. On faith's track the runner dare not slow down after a lap or two, but needs to run full out all the time.

Besides running full out, the serious racer eliminates everything that might hinder him. Extra weight of any kind, whether in the body or in clothing, can only slow the runner down. So the Greek athlete wore only the scantiest of covering. Particularly are we to throw off "the sin that so easily entangles." Like some flopping warm-up robe, sin of any kind can wrap itself around a runner's legs and trip him on the track.

Judas is just one warning example of those who started the race of faith but never finished because of sin's entanglements. From Paul, one of the greatest spiritual athletes ever, comes a positive example. In Philippians 3:13,14 he urges, "One thing I do: Forgetting what is behind and straining toward what is ahead, I press on toward the goal to win the prize for which God has called me heavenward in Christ Jesus."

The Old Testament heroes who ran faith's course successfully can only encourage, but not strengthen us. For ongoing strength and stamina we need to "fix our eyes on Jesus, the author and perfecter of our faith." Again the author uses the present tense in the Greek to remind us to keep fixing our eyes on Jesus. Note also the use of the personal name "Jesus." He's the one who became flesh to furnish our salvation. He's the one who authors, continues and brings our faith to perfection in heaven. From *A* to *Z* he is both the object and the cause of our faith, giving us something to believe and the faith to do so.

What a powerful incentive Jesus' example is for us. He "endured the cross," the author says, using the same root word as for "our perseverance" in verse one. The cross with its torture and disgrace was no light load for our Lord, but he held up under it. The shame involved was far outweighed by the joy he found in completing the work of salvation and sitting down in triumph at God's right hand. In John 17:4 he told his Father with joy, "I have brought you glory on earth by completing the work you gave me to do."

On the last day we shall hear that joy also in the Savior's words to us, "Come, you who are blessed by my Father; take your inheritance, the kingdom prepared for you since the creation of the world" (Matthew 25:34). Why did Jesus endure? Why did he willingly and even joyfully go to cross and tomb? The love and grace involved in the answer leave us speechless. He did it to redeem us.

Such a Jesus the readers are to "consider," looking him over well and checking him from all sides. When feet feel like lead and we think we can't run another step, when hearts are as heavy as our legs and souls are ready to give up, then it's time to consider Jesus. What hostility from sinful men — those very ones he had come to help — our sinless Jesus had to endure. He faced opposition such as those Hebrew readers and we today will never face. Yet undaunted and undismayed he triumphed.

"Keep your eyes fixed on him," the author urges. "Consider him," he advises. Jesus has gone where we are now going and where he is we will be. From him comes not only an example of how to run, but power for faith to pick up the pace and lengthen the stride on the track to heaven.

⁴In your struggle against sin, you have not yet resisted to the point of shedding your blood. ⁵And you have forgotten that word of encouragement that addresses you as sons: "My son, do not make light of the Lord's discipline, and do not lose heart when he rebukes you, ⁶because the Lord disciplines those he loves, and he punishes everyone he accepts as a son."

For Jesus, facing the opposition of men meant the shedding of his blood on Golgotha. For some of the Old Testament heroes there had also been a bloody end, but not so far for the Hebrew Christians. They had had difficult days in the past (10:32-34). Right now they were locked in a struggle with sin as the opponents tried to terrorize them into abandoning their faith in Jesus. Perhaps the future would even demand their blood. Now was no time to be confused or unclear about the role of affliction or as the author calls it, "discipline." So he proceeds with a great section, giving us not all the answers to the problem of suffering, but enough to encourage us to endure.

First of all, the author reminds the readers of what God's word says about discipline. Had they forgotten the word of encouragement recorded in Proverbs 3:11,12? Quoting from the Septuagint, the author shows the close connection God's word makes between sonship and discipline. Discipline is the training necessary to lead a child to maturity. It is the instruction and correction, the leading and warning a father constantly gives his son so that character may be molded and maturity achieved.

Sometimes such discipline comes right from the hand of God. Other times it comes from the hand of the enemy, as for those Hebrew Christians, but with God then shaping it to suit his gracious purposes. But God always sends or bends such discipline for the well-being of his children. That is what it means for him to be our Father and for us to be his children. It means, as Romans 8:28 says so well, that "we know that in all things God works for the good of those who love him."

How shall children react to discipline? "Do not make light of" it, the author urges. When God disciplines, indifference is not a suitable response. God may be saying something important that his children can hear better when shivering in the storm than when basking in the sunshine. To make light of God's discipline might be to miss the message.

Nor are we to "lose heart" because of it. God never forsakes his own. When he tests, he also toughens. However heavy the discipline, his grace will cover. In 1 Corinthians 10:13 Paul comforts us, "God is faithful; he will not let you be tempted beyond what you can bear. But when you are tempted, he will also provide a way out so that you can stand up under it."

The right reaction to God's discipline is confidence in God's love. Those whom he loves he disciplines. Sometimes that even includes flogging with the whip or lash as the word "punish" indicates. Proper training involves both instruction in the way to go and correction when behavior is wayward. Behind such action, too, stands love of the highest kind, as measureless as God himself and magnificent in purpose. From such a loving Father never comes more — or less — discipline than necessary for his children.

7Endure hardship as discipline; God is treating you as sons. For what son is not disciplined by his father? 8If you are not disciplined (and everyone undergoes discipline), then you are illegitimate children and not true sons. 9Moreover, we have all had

human fathers who disciplined us and we respected them for it. How much more should we submit to the Father of our spirits and live!

Secondly, the author reminds the readers more fully of God's care involved in discipline. "Keep enduring hardship as discipline," he urges his readers. Their current troubles were actually for their training and that training was a visible sign that they were God's sons. Aren't fathers supposed to train their sons so they mature instead of remaining childish?

Proverbs 13:24 expresses the same thought, "He who spares the rod hates his son, but he who loves him is careful to discipline him." Only the illegitimate remain untrained because they have no father to care for them. Were the Hebrew readers wearying under and wishing away God's discipline? The lack of discipline may sound good, but in reality it shows a serious problem. It reveals a lack of son-ship and leads to tragic results.

Again the author appeals to the example of our earthly family. "We have all had human fathers who disciplined us," he reminds the readers. Certainly Christian mothers discipline, too, but fathers as heads of the household are finally responsible to God for such disciplining. When that discipline came, perhaps at first we resented it. Later, though, we respected our fathers because we realized what they were trying to do.

How much more should we submit to the heavenly Father, who deals not only with our physical, but also with our spiritual existence! Even when he has to correct us for some fault, it is not to vent his anger, but to reclaim and redirect his wayward sons. This Father has a love which cannot fail and a wisdom which cannot err. To see his caring hand behind life's trials and to submit to his shaping discipline is to live in the fullest sense of the word.

¹⁰Our fathers disciplined us for a little while as they thought best; but God disciplines us for our good, that we may share in his holiness. ¹¹No discipline seems pleasant at the time, but painful. Later on, however, it produces a harvest of righteousness and peace for those who have been trained by it. ¹²Therefore, strengthen your feeble arms and weak knees. ¹³"Make level paths for your feet," so that the lame may not be disabled, but rather healed.

Thirdly, the author reminds the readers more fully of God's purpose involved in discipline. Again he proceeds from the lesser to the greater. Earthly fathers can only discipline "for a little while," only during the brief time their children are growing up. Also earthly fathers can only discipline as they think best, and consequently at times make mistakes.

With God's discipline there is no error, only and always profit for his children. The profit he has in mind is "that we may share in his holiness." "Be perfect, therefore, as your heavenly Father is perfect," Jesus explains in Matthew 5:48. The holy God, who is removed from and reacts against all sin, wants his children to be like him. First he makes them holy by leading them to the Savior. Then he leads them to walk more and more in the holy footsteps of that Savior. Finally, in heaven he crowns them with perfect holiness. How important his discipline becomes when viewed in the light of his gracious purpose.

True, at the time discipline can be painful, but that is because we seldom see the outcome immediately. Like fruit on a tree, the ripening takes time. Those who view the Lord's discipline as the gymnasium for the training of their souls will reap a "harvest of righteousness and peace." Being right with God through faith in Christ's atoning work, they will more and more walk in right conduct toward God. The result is "peace," that little word for that big feeling which comes from knowing sins are pardoned for Christ's sake and lives powered for his service. Such a view of discipline helps rule out faith's complaining and crumbling.

God disciplines in order to strengthen. Those who know this are to put forth their best effort for themselves and for others. With language borrowed from Isaiah 35:3, the author urges his readers, on the brink of spiritual collapse, to reinvigorate limp hands for spiritual battle and lame knees for faith's race. With language borrowed from Proverbs 4:26 he also urges them to " 'make level paths for your feet' so that the lame may not be disabled, but rather healed."

Those who are strengthened by God's discipline are to help clear the track of any obstacles in order to make travel easier for the weak. Lame Christians, not knowing which way to turn and in danger of turning away from Christ, need help from the strong. When the road of faith is rough, as with those Hebrew Christians, the danger that the lame become totally disabled increases alarmingly. That's why the author urges so strongly, "Strengthen your feeble arms and weak knees. 'Make level paths for your feet.' " To the power for such spiritual revitalization he has already pointed by urging all who run the course to keep their eyes fixed on Jesus, the author and perfecter of our faith.

Who of us hasn't tasted God's discipline? Sometimes it comes in sharp and swift doses, almost taking our breath away. Other times it comes in slow and steady waves, almost wearing us out. When it comes, who of us hasn't asked, "Why?" Strangely enough, we can tell our children not to ask why, only to throw that same question at our heavenly Father. Our children are to accept our wisdom as infallible while we feel free to question the ways of the Almighty.

Not *why* but *what* is the proper question when discipline comes. The *why* we have been told often enough and the author of Hebrews has repeated it for us again. It is because our Father loves us and wants to mature us for heaven. The *what* he will show us if we give him time as he strengthens our faith and uses us to strengthen others. Nor will his discipline go on forever. The day will come when he on whom we fix our eyes in faith will return, and when he does, then we shall see face to face and know fully even as we are fully known (1 Corinthians 13:12).

WARNING:
DO NOT REFUSE GOD AT MOUNT ZION AND PERISH

[14]Make every effort to live in peace with all men and to be holy; without holiness no one will see the Lord. [15]See to it that no one misses the grace of God and that no bitter root grows up to cause trouble and defile many. [16]See that no one is sexually immoral, or is godless like Esau, who for a single meal sold his inheritance rights as the oldest son. [17]Afterward, as you know, when he wanted to inherit this blessing, he was rejected. He could bring about no change of mind, though he sought the blessing with tears.

The author still has in mind the race of faith and what we can do to help each other run it. "Make every effort to live in peace," he urges. They were to keep on pursuing peace as runners pursue their goal. This pursuit, difficult already because of man's cantankerous and self-seeking nature, becomes even more arduous when trouble arises. At such times nerves become frayed and frustration is easily vented on those nearest. Persecution was not to produce disharmony among those Hebrew Christians, but make them pursue peace with each other even more earnestly. Isn't this what the Savior encouraged in Matthew 5:9, "Blessed are the peacemakers, for they will be called sons of God"?

The goal was peace toward fellow believers and holiness toward God. Made holy by Jesus' blood and the Spirit's work, believers are now to pursue holiness. More and more, faith is transplanted from the green house of the heart to the garden of daily life. More and more believers strive to walk in the footsteps of their Master. In 2 Corinthians 5:17 Paul tells us, "If anyone is in Christ, he is a new creation; the old has gone, the new has come!" No longer is it life-as-usual, but life-as-Christ-wants.

Such a sanctified life does not come by itself. The believer must pursue it and keep on pursuing it till life's end brings perfect holiness in heaven. When he wearies in the pursuit, he needs to reach for energy from the gospel in word and sacrament. Those who claim to be Christian but show no pursuit of holiness in life have not seen the Lord. Nor will they see him! Like James in 2:20, the author is saying, "Faith without deeds is useless." Jesus Christ is the only ticket to heaven, but our pursuit of holiness is proof that we have been given this ticket by a gracious God.

"See to it," the author continues, using an unusual verb to encourage constant concern for fellow believers. Each believer is to exercise oversight, watching and warning, guiding and guarding lest anyone "miss the grace of God." "Miss" means to drop back on the track. Such lagging behind could be fatal, leading to the loss of God's free gift of salvation. Were some of the Hebrew Christians doing just that, tempted by persecution to drop off the track? Then it was time for the stronger ones to drop back alongside, put the arm around them and encourage them by pointing to the grace of God.

Those who lose God's grace suffer eternal damage for themselves and pose a very real danger for others. In Deuteronomy 29:18 Moses, speaking about defection from the

Lord in the camp of Israel, warned, "Make sure there is no root among you that produces such bitter poison." The author of Hebrews borrows the picture to warn against the same sin. Defection from Christ is like some poisonous root in the ground. Slowly it grows, eventually spreading its contamination also to its surroundings. Were any of those Hebrew Christians thinking of leaving Christ? "Watch out," the author warns. Such defection is contagious. It troubles others and eventually makes them unfit to stand in God's presence when faith is lost.

For an example of what could happen to the readers the author turns to Esau. He describes Esau as "sexually immoral." Because the Old Testament record never connected any act of sexual immorality with Esau, we look for another explanation. Using the picture of sexual unfaithfulness to describe unfaithfulness to God, Judges 2:17 said of Israel, "They prostituted themselves to other gods and worshiped them." Perhaps the author uses the same picture to describe Esau's unfaithfulness to God and his promises.

The author also labels Esau as "godless," a word meaning worldly or profane. Genesis 25:29-34 records an incident which clearly revealed Esau's lack of appreciation for anything spiritual. A dish of red stew for his hungry stomach was more real to him than his rights as the firstborn son and more valuable than the reception of the promise that the Savior would come from his line. His sacred inheritance rights he treated as something common, to be bartered away. Like all the godless, Esau lived for the immediate, not the ultimate.

Wouldn't apostasy by the readers be much the same thing? To leave Christ in order to gain escape from persecution would be like Esau's bartering the ancestorship of Christ for a bowl of stew and a bit of bread. The relief would be immediate, but the ultimate result would be horrible loss.

Esau's warning stands. Afterward, as the readers knew from Genesis 27:30-40, Esau regretted his action and tried to change the mind of his father, Isaac. Though Esau pleaded with bitter tears, he was rejected because the blessing with the promise of the Savior's bloodline had been given to his brother Jacob and could not be returned to him. Nothing is said here about Esau's repentance, only the irreversibility of the damage caused by his actions. What a warning for those tempted to leave Christ! Let them consider the ultimate damage for themselves and others.

[18]You have not come to a mountain that can be touched and that is burning with fire; to darkness, gloom and storm; [19]to a trumpet blast or to such a voice speaking words, so that those who heard it begged that no further word be spoken to them, [20]because they could not bear what was commanded: "If even an animal touches the mountain, it must be stoned." [21]The sight was so terrifying that Moses said, "I am trembling with fear."

The example of Esau's irreversible loss of the promised blessing has set the stage for the final warning section of this epistle. Throughout the letter the author's aim has been to win loyalty from his readers for a superior Christ and to warn them against leaving his better covenant. One more time the author sounds the warning, summarized in the earnest plea, "See to it that you do not refuse him (God) who speaks."

This section, contrasting the old and new covenants, is one of the most dramatic in the Bible. Vividly the author shows what believers in Christ would give up if they returned to Judaism. First he takes the reader back to Mt. Sinai where the Mosaic Law was given. He echoes words from Exodus 19-20 and Deuteronomy 5 where the terrifying scenes at Sinai were recorded. Mt. Sinai was earthly and touchable; it still stands rugged and real in the desert.

What happened at that mountain was completely unearthly! The blazing fire, the thick smoke, the impenetrable blackness, the howling whirlwind, the escalating trumpet blasts, awed the people, filling them with a deep sense of God's presence and power. To people already trembling the sound of God's voice speaking the commandments was too much. They begged Moses, "Speak to us yourself and we will listen. But do not have God speak to us or we will die" (Exodus 20:19).

Their fear was heightened by the commands God had given in Exodus 19:9-13 concerning their conduct for this awesome event. Only one of the divine edicts is mentioned here, a command which completely unnerved them. Any animal which touched the mountain was to be stoned. The people were not even to touch the straying animal but rather kill it by throwing stones or shooting darts at it (Exodus 19:13).

If that was the penalty for an uncomprehending animal, what about those who could grasp the warning? The entire scene at Sinai was so filled with fear and foreboding that Moses, their leader and God's friend, himself was shaking. His exact words, "I am trembling with fear," are not recorded in the Old Testament account at Sinai, so evidently Moses was included in the statement in Exodus 19:16 that "everyone in the camp trembled." All who witnessed the giving of the Law at Sinai were awed by the supernatural demonstration of God's holiness and power.

Is that what the readers wanted? Did they really want to return to Judaism with its old covenant of the law? The law with its thunder and trumpets can provide no pardon for sin-troubled hearts or peace for sin-torn consciences. All it offers is the awesome revelation of God's righteous requirements and the horrible fear of his just punishment over infractions. All it can do is point out the impassable and impossible distance sin puts between man and God, but the law can offer nothing to bridge the gap.

There is no future at Mt. Sinai, no access to God, no acceptance by God, no eternity with God. And yet men try! Misled by the devil, misguided by their own conceit, even misinformed by their churches, they dare to think they can approach a holy God by means of what they do. What tragedy to try to touch a holy God in this way only to receive eternal death in hell!

22But you have come to Mount Zion, to the heavenly Jerusalem, the city of the living God. You have come to thousands upon thousands of angels in joyful assembly, 23to the church of the firstborn, whose names are written in heaven. You have come to God, the judge of all men, to the spirits of righteous men made perfect, 24to Jesus the mediator of a new covenant, and to the sprinkled blood that speaks a better word than the blood of Abel.

"But" the author begins the marked contrast. "You have come," he reminds his readers, pointing out how far they have been carried and where they are now standing by the grace of God. Already they have come "to Mount Zion." Zion was one of the hills on which Jerusalem had been built and is used here to refer to heaven, the dwelling place of the Most High. Already on earth the believer owns heaven; already today he possesses tomorrow. There in Zion stands the "heavenly Jerusalem, the city of the living God." In Zion stands the city of which the earthly Jerusalem was but a faint shadow. There dwells the living God in the eternal city of which he is both architect and builder.

In that city we have grand company. There are "the thousands upon thousands of angels in joyful assembly." The angels were there on Sinai sharing in the solemn giving of the Law as Galatians 3:19 records. To earth the Father sends them to serve those who "will inherit salvation" as already mentioned in 1:14. But in heaven they join in festal assembly to marvel at God's love for sinners. Revelation 5:12 records their festive song, "Worthy is the Lamb, who was slain, to receive power and wealth and wisdom and strength and honor and glory and praise!" Already on earth, though off key, believers join the angels in that hymn of praise to be sung eventually in heaven's perfect harmony.

Believers have more companions, for they are part of "the church of the firstborn, whose names are written in heaven." All believers have the rank of firstborn in God's sight. They are heirs of his salvation with all that it offers. God has entered their names in his heavenly family record even more carefully than the Jews did in their earthly genealogical records.

Scripture loves that expression: "written in heaven." In Luke 10:20 Jesus told his disciples, "Rejoice that your names are written in heaven," and in Philippians 4:3 Paul spoke of fellow workers "whose names are in the book of life." Each believer carries citizenship papers for heaven written in the indelible ink of God's grace. Every believer on earth has a room reserved in the Father's house.

The mention of "God, the judge of all men" in the middle of this glorious scene need not trouble the believer. Let those fear who would despise or desert his grace. He will judge all men and do it justly. But those who stand before him as his firstborn sons, clothed with his Son's righteousness, need not fear. When we pass the judgment, we will join "the spirits of righteous men made perfect." To stand beside Moses and Abraham, to listen to Paul and John, to speak with Luther and our forefathers, will be heavenly indeed. The souls of those righteous believers have reached the perfect goal of heaven even though we wait for the ancient graves to yield up their bodies.

Without Jesus and his blood of the new covenant we would have no free access to the Father's throne, no inheritance in the Father's house, no company with rejoicing angels, no fellow believers as companions along the way, no mercy in the judgment, no hope beyond the grave. No wonder the author ends the list of blessings his readers have received as believers by pointing to "Jesus the mediator of a new covenant, and to the sprinkled blood that speaks a better word than the blood of Abel."

"Jesus," he calls him, reminding us of how God came into the flesh to save us. He also describes Jesus as mediator of a new covenant, taking us back to 8:6. Jesus is the go-between who put God's covenant of grace into effect by the shedding of his precious blood. While the spilt blood of Abel in Genesis 4:10 is described as crying out to God for vengeance, Christ's blood sprinkling the sinner speaks of pardon and peace. For the last of twelve times in all, the author uses the word "better," this time to describe the blessed gospel message of forgiveness spoken by Jesus' blood.

What would it be for the readers? Sinai or Zion? The law's loud thunder or the gospel's tender love? The law's curse, "Your iniquities have separated you from your God" (Isaiah 59:2) or the gospel's inviting cry, "Come, for everything is now ready" (Luke 14:17)? The catastrophe of an endless hell or the consummation of an everlasting heaven? The answer is found only in the gospel message of Jesus' blood and in faith worked by the Spirit through that message. God help us day by day to fill faith's lungs with heaven's pure air even as we pray, "Jesus, in mercy bring us to that dear land of rest, who art with God the Father and Spirit, ever blest."

²⁵See to it that you do not refuse him who speaks. If they did not escape when they refused him who warned them on earth, how much less will we, if we turn away from him who warns us from heaven? ²⁶At that time his voice shook the earth, but now he has promised, "Once more I will shake not only the earth, but also the heavens." The words "once more" indicate the removing of what can be shaken — that is, created things — so that what cannot be shaken may remain. ²⁸Therefore, since we are receiving a kingdom that cannot be shaken, let us be thankful, and so worship God acceptably with reverence and awe, for our God is a consuming fire.

Greater privilege involves greater responsibility. To abuse greater privilege results in greater blame. God spoke both at Mt. Sinai on earth in the law and from the heavenly Mt. Zion in the gospel. Those who refused to hear what he had said in the law soon found out how serious he was. When Israel said no to the Lord and his commandments, such as with their worship of the golden calf and incident after incident during their wilderness trek, they did not escape. Their bones were laid in desert graves and they lost also the heavenly Canaan.

The Hebrew Christians had heard God "warn" or speak divine communications to them from heaven. What this means Peter explains in 2 Peter 1:12 by describing the gospel as being preached "by the Holy Spirit sent from heaven." The gospel is God's voice from heaven. Through it his Spirit pleads in love, wooing and winning the hearts of sinners with love's great power. To refuse him when he speaks in tender love is to be more reprehensible than those who refused the thunder of his law. For such there is no escape from damnation because there is no other provision for sin. Turning it around, what the author urges those Hebrew Christians to do is to listen more closely and cling more tightly to the better message of Christ's pardon and peace.

Moreover, the voice that now speaks from Calvary with gospel grace will speak again. On Sinai when he spoke, the mountain shook. Exodus 19:18 records how "the Lord descended on it in fire" and how "the whole mountain trembled violently." But that stupendous earth-shaking was nothing compared to what was coming. In Haggai 2:6 the Lord gave his promise which still stands, as the author reveals by quoting it in free form. Once more the Lord will do some shaking. When Christ returns on the Last Day, not only the earth, but heavens around it will rock and reel. The "created things" which seemed so permanent will perish. All the shaken things will be removed. "That day will bring about the destruction of the heavens by fire," 2 Peter 3:12 says, "and the elements will melt in the heat."

Only that "which cannot be shaken" will remain. The author does not explain what the unshaken thing is. He has already told us earlier. It is the heavenly Jerusalem, the city with foundations, Mt. Zion, where the living God dwells and where all his children will live with him forever.

Dare any reader refuse to listen to the voice of such a King poised for that last great act? Turning it around, what the author tells his readers is to listen more closely and cling more tightly to that gospel word from heaven so that they might be part of that which will remain eternally unshaken in that Last Great Day.

Once more the author reminds his readers of what they have. Judaism with its outward ritual and outdated Mosaic Covenant were things that could be shaken. But the treasures they had already received in Christ and the eternal heavenly kingdom already theirs in part would not, in fact, "cannot" pass away. There could be only one proper reaction for such an unshakable treasure. Not to trifle with or toss it aside, but to "be thankful" and to show that thankfulness in worshiping "God acceptably with reverence and awe." The word "worship" is wider, including service in general. The grateful believer offers his life in service to God with reverence, with eyes cast down humbly in the presence of a holy God. He offers it also with awe, with diligent concern for avoiding whatever might displease his Lord.

It is a solemn appeal the author puts before us, combining both faith and fear. Those who possess the unshakable kingdom have no business dallying around or dividing their loyalty. It is all or nothing for God, who has given us all and promised us even more. "Our God is a consuming fire," the author somberly concludes quoting from Deuteronomy 4:24 where Moses had warned Israel never to leave the Lord and lapse into idolatry.

But even as the author warns us against deterioration and defection, we note his gospel tone. "Our God," he calls him. His consuming fire of judgment comes only if we won't let him be our God. To trifle with his grace is to receive his fiery wrath. To live in his grace is to live forever.

"Today if you hear his voice, do not harden your hearts" (3:8,15; 4:7).

Let Us Live in Faith Toward Those Around Us

13 **Keep on loving each other as brothers. ²Do not forget to entertain strangers, for by so doing some people have entertained angels without knowing it. ³Remember those in prison as if you were their fellow prisoners, and those who are mistreated as if you yourselves were suffering.**

Christ and covenant, faith and fear have been well covered by the author. Now follows a concluding section which he has packed full of practical applications about

169

faith in action and love at work. "Keep on loving each other as brothers," he begins, highlighting the section. The flame of brotherly love had been showing in their midst; it was surely not to go out now. Where persecution strikes, brotherly love has a hard time staying lit as people pull back, cautious about identity and concerned about safety. So the author urges them to practice the kind of love and concern you would expect toward those born from the same womb.

Much more is that kindness and helpfulness to show among those born of the same Spirit. Jesus himself said so. In John 13:34 he told his disciples on Maundy Thursday, "A new commandment I give you: Love one another." The apostles repeated it. Paul in 1 Thessalonians 4:9 reminded his readers, "You yourselves have been taught by God to love each other." In 1 Peter 1:22 that apostle urged, "Love one another deeply, from the heart." And that great apostle of love who repeated it again and again, summarized in 1 John 3:11, "This is the message you heard from the beginning: We should love one another."

Do we need the reminder? What do we see as we look around at fellow believers? What do we see when we look at ourselves and our attitudes and actions toward fellow believers? Is it love for him as a brother and desire to help him succeed or self-centered thoughts that cause heated competition with him? Is it brotherly concern for his needs or calloused seeking of our own good? Is it acceptance of his talents and assistance in developing them or caustic criticism of what he says and does? Brotherly love such as our Lord asks of us requires constant practice and concentrated power that can come only from the cross of our Elder Brother.

Such love shows not only toward those known and near, but also to strangers. In the ancient world where inns weren't that plentiful nor their reputations that pure, hospitality was a prized virtue. Christians who were forced to flee from their towns because of persecution or who went traveling on a preaching mission were particularly in need of hospitality. They would benefit greatly as would also those extending the hospitality. Great was Abraham's benefit in Genesis 18:3 and Lot's in 19:2 when the strangers they invited into their homes turned out to be angels.

We shall probably never entertain angels when we help strangers. Although it is becoming increasingly difficult to help strangers, let us not forget the value our Lord himself places on such Christian hospitality. What a surprise it will be to hear from him on the Last Day, "Whatever you did for one of the least of these brothers of mine, you did for me" (Matthew 25:40). Also as fellow believers move and travel more, let us make sure our churches are warm with hospitality. Let us welcome strangers to our services and new members to our midst warmly instead of watching them warily from a distance.

Not only were strangers to receive brotherly love, so should sufferers. The prisoner and the persecuted need more than pity; they need love which can feel with them and then act for them. 1 Corinthians 12:26 describes Christians as forming a body where "if one part suffers, every part suffers with it." The Hebrew Christians had responded in just that way in earlier days of persecution as 10:32-34 has pointed out. They were not to stop now in showing sympathy to suffering saints.

Certainly it is easier to shut our eyes and ears to the needs of our brethren. It may even appear safer to join the priest and the Levite in the Good Samaritan parable and pass by on the other side. But that's not brotherly love! Believers ridiculed in university lecture rooms, ostracized by unbelieving families, brave enough to stand up for Christian principles on the job, need more than our silent applause. They need our strengthening love.

⁴Marriage should be honored by all, and the marriage bed kept pure, for God will judge the adulterer and all the sexually immoral. ⁵Keep your lives free from the love of money and be content with what you have, because God has said, "Never will I leave you; never will I forsake you." ⁶So we say with confidence, "The Lord is my helper; I will not be afraid. What can man do to me?"

The author turns to another area where love is expressed, to marriage and particularly the marriage bed. The heathen world needed to be told that marriage was God's institution, given, governed and guarded by him. Even before sin's entrance it was there, but sin has stained marriage and sullied the marriage bed. "Honored by all," the author urges, but what God gave as a precious gift is downgraded, disgraced, and discarded. The gift of sex brings blessings only in the marriage bed. Those who would defile it outside of marriage will be judged. Human courts may allow and human eyes may not see, but God will certainly see and relentlessly judge every violation. Let the church bravely proclaim God's holy will in this vital area even when most of the world doesn't want to hear it. Let the believer find power to swim against the present tide of immorality and be blessed by God.

Next the author speaks about another love, only this time in warning. "Keep your lives free from the love of money," he urges. From warning against immorality he turns to the love of money. Quite naturally so, for Scripture often links these two together (1 Corinthians 5:11, Ephesians 5:3). A covetous person pays little attention to anyone else's well-being as he selfishly pursues his own aims, be they sexual or financial. Christians are to keep their lives, their way of thinking and living, free from such money love. Those who don't, those whose greedy hearts and grasping fingers reach more for gold than for God, would do well to remember Paul's warning in 1 Timothy 6:10: "Some people, eager for money, have wandered from the faith and pierced themselves with many griefs."

The antidote is to "be content" with what we have. Christians believe that God knows what is best for them. Whatever they have they regard as having come from him, to be managed for him. And there they stop! To go beyond invites either sinful worry or ungodly greed. In a world which revolves around the possessions you have and the position you hold it is not easy to practice contentment. It is not easy to join Paul in the words of Philippians 4:11: "I have learned to be content whatever the circumstances."

What is the secret of contentment? The author points it out. It is to remember our God's promise, "Never will I leave you; never will I forsake you." First given to Joshua as he took over Moses' heavy mantle (Deuteronomy 31:6, Joshua 1:5), this gracious promise applies also to us. Never will he leave or fail to uphold us. Never will he forsake or abandon us. Always he goes with us. Always he is our eternal Resource. What more could we ever want? Constant mindfulness of God's fatherly presence and of his never-failing promises is the key to contentment.

When God speaks, the believer responds. With confident courage he declares on the basis of Psalm 118:6, "The Lord is my helper, I will not be afraid, what can man do to me?" Content with God's perfect provision, covered with God's perfect protection, the believer walks toward heaven's shores unafraid. He knows that with God on his side he has a

173

majority of one, regardless what foes or fears he faces. Were those Hebrew Christians, afraid of persecution, listening? Are we?

⁷Remember your leaders, who spoke the word of God to you. Consider the outcome of their way of life and imitate their faith. ⁸Jesus Christ is the same yesterday and today and forever. ⁹Do not be carried away by all kinds of strange teachings. It is good for our hearts to be strengthened by grace, not by ceremonial foods, which are of no value to those who eat them.

The author never loses sight of his goal. Weakening Christians were to be encouraged, wandering ones warned. That is why he points his readers back to their former leaders. "Keep on remembering your leaders who spoke the word of God to you," he urges. Their faithful proclamation of divine truth had brought the readers much benefit in the past. Benefit could be had also in the present time of persecution by thinking back to those leaders and their teachings.

"Consider the outcome of their way of life," he also urged. The readers were to scan carefully the faithful life and fearless death of their past leaders. Whether death had come from martyrdom or natural causes, their falling asleep in Jesus provided inspiration for all, especially for those facing violence by persecution.

The author further urged, "Keep imitating their faith." Those leaders had been true to Christ up to the end. None had weakened or wavered in the faith as some of the readers were now tempted to do. Here were examples for the Jewish Christians to consider and follow. Have we had such faithful leaders? Then thank God for them! Only such faithful leaders deserve to be followed. God help us imitate them!

The former leaders are gone, but what they taught and believed remains eternally the same. Their Savior is our Savior and will be our children's Savior. He is always the believer's contemporary. What he did for believers in the past, he will do for us. What he does for us, he will do for those who follow us. Note his full name — "Jesus" to refer to God come in the flesh to save us and "Christ" to refer to his great office of prophet, priest and king. The winds of time invariably shift the sands of earth but leave the eternal Savior untouched. Jesus Christ and all that he offers, Jesus Christ and all that he promises, "is the same yesterday and today and forever." Believers of any century have but one ground for their faith and goal for their life, "Jesus Christ."

The author follows with a warning about teaching anything other than the eternal Christ and his changeless word. Such a warning was in place, for the readers were in danger of being carried off course "by all kinds of strange teaching." What these various false teachings, foreign to the gospel, were we are not specifically told. Both the author and the readers knew what was meant. The phrase "ceremonial foods" seems to indicate some promotion of Judaism at the expense of Christianity. For Jewish Christians facing persecution because of Christ and his word, Judaism with its many rituals seemed to offer a safe and satisfying retreat. But the author warns them such action would be listening to the wrong things and following the wrong track. Ceremonial foods have no value for the heart. Holiness comes not from outward ritual, but from Christ's redeeming work and God's sanctifying grace.

Did those readers need strengthening for their faith? In John 17:17 the Savior in his prayer to the Father for believers shows the only way. "Sanctify them by the truth; your word is truth," he prayed. Only God's grace can strengthen the inner life of man and it does so only through the word. Do we desire strengthening of faith? Then it's to the word, the eternal gospel of God's grace!

¹⁰We have an altar from which those who minister at the tabernacle have no right to eat. ¹¹The high priest carries the blood of animals into the Most Holy Place as a sin offering, but the bodies are burned outside the camp. ¹²And so Jesus also suffered outside the city gate to make the people holy through his own blood. ¹³Let us, then, go to him outside the camp, bearing the disgrace he bore. ¹⁴For here we do not have an enduring city, but we are looking for the city that is to come.

What did those Jewish Christians want with Judaism? Were they looking for visible temples, altars and sacrifices? Then let them consider what they had now in Christianity. "We HAVE an altar," the author points out triumphantly. That altar is the cross where Christ sacrificed himself and secured eternal salvation for us. Those who still want to "minister at the tabernacle," that is, cling in worship to the old rituals connected with Judaism, have no right to the blessings of the cross. Ceremonial foods mean more to them than God's grace in Christ.

Once more the author points to Christ and his better sacrifice. Jesus' cross and his sacrifice on that cross are all that anyone needs. Even the great Old Testament Day of Atonement had foreshadowed this. On that day, as we have already heard earlier in the epistle, the high priest carried into the Most Holy Place the blood of a bullock as offering for his own sins and the blood of a goat as offering for the people's sins. But on the altar of the cross the blood from Emmanuel's veins flowed in a single, satisfactory sacrifice for all sins. On the Day of Atonement after that animal blood had been sprinkled on the mercy seat, the bodies were burned outside the camp (Leviticus 16:27). That smoldering fire outside the camp reminded Israel of sin's removal.

What a shadow of Jesus! His cross stood outside the city gate. John 19:20 describes it as "near the city." The cross itself was a sign of sin's horribleness as Galatians 3:13 reminds us, "Cursed is everyone who is hung on a tree." That cross outside the city gates speaks of deepest disgrace, but its blessed results are forever. By his blood, unlike the gallons of animal blood shed over the years, people are made holy. Jesus' sacrifice on Calvary's cross did what those repeated animal sacrifices could never do. It brought people out of a sinful world and into God's holy family.

Leave such an altar with such a wonderful sacrifice? No, the author instead issues the bold call, "Let us, then, go to him outside the camp, bearing the disgrace he bore." Judaism has nothing to offer to believers who know about Jesus and his all-sufficient cross. To revert to Judaism would mean to leave the cross and lose its benefits. The break with Judaism was vital, but dangerous. Identifying with Christ in faith would mean also "bearing the disgrace he bore." Gentiles would persecute them and fellow Jews would revile them as renegades to the God and faith of their fathers.

But this bold step of faith was well worth it as the author has argued all along. Ahead lay the heavenly Jerusalem with its inheritance which 1 Peter 1:4 said, "can never perish, spoil, or fade." This is the magnet drawing the believer's eyes of faith ever upward. Persecution may bruise his back, but dare not slow his step. Reproach may bring tears to the eyes, but dare not tear those eyes away from heaven's shores. How foolish to trade in such a treasure for a handful of sand and a moment of safety!

Are 20th century believers listening? Have we felt the stones of sarcasm and the sharp arrows of ridicule? Have we found out how thin faith's skin is and how easily it bruises? Have we discovered that the Master knew what he was talking about when he said in Matthew 16:24, "If anyone would come after me, he must deny himself and take up his cross and follow me"? Perhaps it is time to recheck our hearts and lives carefully. Perhaps it is time to hear again the author's urgent call, "Let us, then, go to HIM outside the camp."

¹⁵Through Jesus, therefore, let us continually offer to God a sacrifice of praise — the fruit of lips that confess his name. ¹⁶And do not forget to do good and to share with others, for with such sacrifices God is pleased.

Those who stand in faith beneath Christ's cross realize there is no more need for sin-offerings. They do, however, feel the need for other offerings. Grateful love compels them to respond with willing thank offerings. Nor will such offerings be limited to set times and specified occasions. They will rather rise continually to God. First the author mentions the "sacrifice of praise — the fruit of lips that confess his name." "Out of the overflow of the heart the mouth speaks," Jesus observed in Matthew 12:34. That's how it is with praise. Praise is the believer's heart rising with its hallelujahs to a gracious God. You don't have to pressure praise out of the heart or paste it on the lips. Like fruit it ripens automatically.

Particularly does praise show in bold confession of Jesus' name. "Look what Jesus has done for me, look what he would do for you," faith boldly confesses. What a reminder for those who because of persecution were tempted to grow quiet about or even go away from that Savior and what he offered. What a reminder for us who have so much for which to praise him and so many to whom to confess his saving name!

From unashamed confession the author turns to compassionate service. Fruit shows not only on the lips, but in lives. "Do not forget," the author says, "to do good and to share with others." "To do good" is general, reminding us that whatever we do for anyone else is to be well done. "To share" is more specific, including tangibles like our money and goods and intangibles like comfort for the sorrowing and concern for the troubled. Words of praise and works of love are sacrifices pleasing to God, but only "through Jesus" as the author reminds us by placing that telling phrase emphatically at the front of the verse.

Only through Jesus can hearts become grateful hearts. Only through Jesus do grateful hearts become offering hearts. And only through Jesus are the impurities that still cling to the offerings we bring sifted out so that God is well pleased. "I am the vine; you are the branches," the Savior said similarly in John 15:5, "If a man remains in me and I in him, he will bear much fruit; apart from me you can do nothing."

17Obey your leaders and submit to their authority. They keep watch over you as men who must give an account. Obey them so that their work will be a joy, not a burden, for that would be of no advantage to you.

In verse seven the author urged remembrance of past leaders. Now he turns to present leaders and has something to say about them. "Keep on obeying them," he commands, "keep on submitting to their authority." Though Scripture says much about spiritual leaders, their qualifications and responsibilities, it has little to say about our reactions to them. So we listen to this verse with extra attention.

We are to obey our leaders, something not difficult to do when we agree with them. We are even to do that which is harder, submit to their authority when we don't agree with them. Evidently the spiritual leaders of those Hebrew Christians had remained true teachers and staunch confessors of

Christ and were thus deserving of such obedience. We can well imagine that the author was urging his readers to follow their leaders and heed their warnings against forsaking Christ for the supposed safety of Judaism.

Proper reaction to leaders was necessary for as the author pointed out, "They keep watch over you as men who must give an account." Like caring shepherds, those leaders kept sleepless vigil over every sheep in the flock, guiding them to the pasture of the word, guarding them against sin's danger, gently handling the weak and the wounded, going lovingly after the straying. Each soul was precious to them; for each soul they had to give an account to the Chief Shepherd.

Such awesome responsibility challenges the shepherd, demanding that he give the best he can in every sermon and lesson, every visit and contact. Such serious responsibility also makes demands on every sheep in the flock. When the sheep follow willingly, the shepherd's task is joyful. When they balk or even disobey, the shepherd's joy turns into groaning, and forward motion for the flock slows or even stops. "That would be of no advantage to you," the author warns the flock to which he is writing.

God preserve us from shepherds who watch more for their own fame or finances than for the flock. God preserve us from being sheep who follow only when they feel like it and who obey only when they want to. God give us faithful shepherds and obedient sheep.

Personal Instructions and Final Greetings

[18]Pray for us. We are sure that we have a clear conscience and desire to live honorably in every way. [19]I particularly urge you to pray so that I may be restored to you soon. [20]May the God of peace, who through the blood of the eternal covenant brought back from the dead our Lord Jesus, that great Shepherd of sheep,

The Good Shepherd

²¹equip you with everything good for doing his will, and may he work in us what is pleasing to him, through Jesus Christ, to whom be glory for ever and ever. Amen.

The author has rebuked his readers sharply and warned them intensely. But he still considers them God's children and his own brothers. So he appeals for their continued prayers. "Keep on praying for us," he urges, desiring their prayers both for himself and for his fellow workers. Particularly does he request their prayers for his speedy restoral to them.

Some force outside his control had taken him away from those Hebrew Christians. Could it have been imprisonment, sickness, another mission? We are not told. But he did greatly desire to be back with them and they needed his presence as the contents of his letter have shown.

Also it appears that some of them were leveling criticism at him and his helpers. Perhaps those who advocated Judaism found it advantageous to criticize the author's actions and motives. If so, then the author's reference to a "clear conscience" and a "desire to live honorably in every way" would be explained. Here was a leader who with a clean conscience could wholeheartedly ask his people to pray for him.

Here was also a leader who knew how to pray for his people. Briefly and beautifully he sums up the whole epistle in the form of a fervent prayer for them. In just one sentence he wishes for them all that Christ has to offer. Christianity has the "God of peace." Yes, he is the great Judge who will shake heaven and earth with his terror, but for us he is the God of our salvation. From him comes the peace "which transcends all understanding" (Philippians 4:7), the peace which restless hearts have to have, the peace of restored fellowship with God.

Vividly and clearly the author once more reminds the readers how God brought about this peace. He points them to "our Lord Jesus," linking his own faith with that of his readers in the Savior, who was both divine "Lord" and human "Jesus." This Savior God brought back from the dead through the blood of the eternal covenant. The author has frequently spoken about "covenant" in his letter, but this is the first time he mentions Christ's resurrection. Note how closely he connects the two. Christ's blood, shed on Calvary's cross, paid sin's penalty and established God's covenant of salvation. But that precious blood would have been wasted in Calvary's dust if Christ had remained in the grave. His resurrection from the dead is living proof that sin has been paid for and heaven opened. The filled cross and the emptied tomb are the seals of our salvation. Such a covenant of grace is eternal, never requiring updating or replacing.

Also this is the only time the author refers to Jesus as "Shepherd." The "great" Shepherd he even calls him because with his death and resurrection Jesus has earned the highest rank. This Shepherd believers can trust completely, even when persecution strikes. The bleeding Shepherd is one who will lead and feed them till they reach "the springs of living water," where "God will wipe away every tear from their eyes" (Revelation 7:17).

To the God of peace who had done so much for them in Christ the author prays, "May (he) equip you with everything good for doing his will, and may he work in us what is pleasing to him." Doing God's will and working what is pleasing to God are life's main concerns. God's will is that sinners repent and live. God's will is also that sinners then strive in thankful faith to follow his holy commandments.

All this sounds so easy and yet is so impossible for man. Only as God equips, only as he plants faith in man's heart and powers that faith into daily living, can man follow. In Philippians 2:13 Paul said the same thing: "It is God who works in you to will and to act according to his good purpose." The faith God requires he gives through his grace in word and sacrament. The fruit he looks for on the tree of faith he also grows through the same grace.

"Through Jesus Christ," the author reminded his readers one last time. Not through Mosaic covenants and animal sacrifices, but through Jesus Christ does God give pardon, peace and power. To that perfect Savior belongs all the glory for ever and ever. Heaven's halls will ring with the eternal song, "To him who loves us and has freed us from our sins by his blood, and has made us to be a kingdom and priests to serve his God and Father — to him be glory and power for ever and ever!" (Revelation 1:5,6). God grant that all past and present readers of this epistle be there to echo faith's triumphant "Amen."

22Brothers, I urge you to bear with my word of exhortation, for I have written you only a short letter. 23I want you to know that our brother Timothy has been released. If he arrives soon, I will come with him to see you. 24Greet all your leaders and all God's people. Those from Italy send you their greetings.

His prayer ended, the author pens a conclusion. First he shows concern about the readers' reaction to his letter. He has written at some length and yet calls the letter "short" because of the momentous matters it has covered. He has written in a straightforward manner and even sharply at times and yet does not want the readers to rebel. Affectionately now as to brothers, he appeals for acceptance of his word of exhortation. Like some pastor who in concern has delivered a timely sermon, he desires but one reaction, for believers to accept and follow the truth.

He also had some news for them about Timothy, well-known to them. Timothy had been released either from some prison or some mission and would soon be back with the author. Then together they could come back to the readers. Meanwhile, those receiving this letter were to greet both their leaders and all God's people, an expression common in the early church for believers. "Those from Italy" also sent greetings along with the author. To some this expression seems to indicate believers from Italy now living outside of that country, sending greetings back to their mother church in Rome. From where we cannot say for certain, but believers concerned about each other's spiritual well-being were sending greetings to fellow believers.

25Grace be with you all.

This final verse, found in various forms in many of the New Testament epistles, is more than our conventional "truly yours" closing. It is a prayer that God's undeserved favor in Christ Jesus would rest in full upon all the readers. What a fitting close for a letter so filled with the message of that rich grace in Christ!

So ends our journey through one of the deepest and richest books of the New Testament. God grant that our study has reminded us again what a supreme treasure we have in Christ and what we are to do with this supreme treasure.

To him be glory
for ever and ever.
Amen.